A CHRONICLE OF WAR OF 1812 SOLDIERS, SEAMEN, AND MARINES

1993 EDITION
with added
YEAR 2000 SUPPLEMENT

The emblem of the Society of the War of 1812 in Maryland
as it first appeared June 1, 1908

BATTLE MONUMENT, BALTIMORE.

The cornerstone of the Battle Monument was laid on September 12, 1815 at the occasion of the first Defenders' Day observance. Many veterans subscribed to the expense of the shaft and were released from their labors on that date to witness and to participate in the ceremonies. It continues to be the focus of Baltimore's Defenders' Day commemoration. The engraving above dates from 1825, the year the monument was completed.

A CHRONICLE
OF WAR OF 1812 SOLDIERS, SEAMEN, AND MARINES

1993 EDITION
with added
YEAR 2000 SUPPLEMENT

by
DENNIS F. BLIZZARD
and
THOMAS L. HOLLOWAK

MARYLAND SOCIETY OF THE WAR OF 1812

CLEARFIELD

A Chronicle of War of 1812 Soldiers, Seamen and Marines
originally published Westminster, Maryland, 1993
Copyright © 1993 by the
Society of the War of 1812 in Maryland of Baltimore City, Inc.
All Rights Reserved.

Added Year 2000 Supplement
Copyright © 2001 by the
Society of the War of 1812 in Maryland of Baltimore City, Inc.
All Rights Reserved.

Reprinted, two volumes in one, with the permission of the
Society of the War of 1812 in Maryland of Baltimore City, Inc.,
for Clearfield Company, Inc., by
Genealogical Publishing Co., Inc.
Baltimore, Maryland
2001

International Standard Book Number: 0-8063-5105-5

Made in the United States of America

(Real measures were taken to reproduce names and data as discernible from original manuscripts. The publisher accepts no responsibility for omissions, misstatements, or other inaccuracies which may or may not appear in this book.)

CONTENTS

Prologue x

History of the Society of the War of 1812 xiii

Preface xvii

Introduction 1

Chronicle of Soldiers, Seamen, and Marines 3

Index 115

Appendix 131
    Officers of the Society 133
    Records and Documents 138
    Commemorations 138

YEAR 2000 SUPPLEMENT

Preface to Supplement 141

Notes 142

Chronicle of Soldiers, Sailors, and Marines (Supplement) 143

Member Index (Supplement) 151

Other Names Index (Supplement) 151

*The Society of the War of 1812
in the
State of Maryland
requests the honor of your company
at the dinner to be given to the
General Society of the War of 1812
convening in
Biennial Congress in Baltimore
on the evening of September twelfth
nineteen hundred and fourteen
at seven o'clock
Hotel Belvedere*

LIST OF ILLUSTRATIONS

Battle Monument, Baltimore   ii

1914 Invitation   vi

Rogers' Bastion Number 4   viii

Fort McHenry   ix

Preamble   xi

Steamboat   xii

Old Defenders' Reunion   xvi

Rogers' Bastion Number 4 on an eminence at the eastern edge of the City of Baltimore looks out over the road to North Point and the Patapsco River. The man on the right points in the direction of the British movement up the North Point neck after disembarkation from the river shown in midground of the sketch. In front of this position Colonel Brooke, who succeeded General Ross, encamped the night of September 12, after the previous afternoon engagement at North Point. On September 13, the enemy began to retire toward North Point, which lies to the right of the plume of smoke. From Benson J. Lossing, *The Pictorial Field-Book of the War of 1812*, New York, 1868.

FORT M'HENRY, BALTIMORE HARBOR, MD.

The shelling of Fort McHenry was intended as a diversionary offensive for Ross' assult by land, as well as a marine reprisal against Baltimore's shipping and priveteering. The North Point effort was not abandonded at the time that the demonstration upon the fort commenced at six-thirty in the morning of September 13. The bombardment continued until the early hours of the following day. The British vessels returned to a safe distance during September 14, and moved out of the harbor entrance two days later. The fort's casualties were 4 killed and 24 wounded. The early 19th century engraving is unattributable. In the sketch Baltimore lies about two miles, left and to the rear.

PROLOGUE

The enemy have been compelled to retire from before this City, the Major General commanding takes pleasure in congratulating the troops under his command, upon a relaxtion of those severe duties to which they submitted to privations of every kind was as gratifying to him as the alacrity with which they flew to arms for the protection of the city.

Major General Samuel Smith
General Order of 19 September 1814

****

Intelligence of the defense of Baltimore was received throughout the country with every demonstration of joy. The joy of the Baltimoreans, rescued, as it seemed to them, from the very jaws of destruction, cannot be described. Measures were taken for a perpetual celebration of the event; rewards were proposed for those who had filled distinguished positions in the defense; and a beautiful monument in the centre of the city perpetuates the names and memory of those who fell in defense of their homes. Around it, on each returning anniversary of the day, amid dense crowds of spectators, the pomp of military escort and the stirring strains of martial music, march, under a tattered flag, a handful of aged men, their number lessening every year, the survivors of that eventful 12th of September, the honored company of *Old Defenders*. May it yet be long ere the last survivor of that venerable band performs his solitary circuit.

J. Thomas Scharf
History of Baltimore City and County, 1881

****

Commemorating the centennial of the incorporation of the Maryland Society, this book has been prepared to contain military and personal data on veterans and their descendants. As a work in American history and genealogy, it stands as a source to guide future research.

Henry C. Peden, Jr.
Genealogist, Society of the War of 1812 in Maryland

PREAMBLE

HEREAS, in the Providence of God, victory having crowned the forces of the United States of America, in upholding the principles of the Nation against Great Britain in the conflict known as the War of 1812; we the survivors and descendants of those who participated in that contest, have joined together to perpetuate its memories and victories; to collect and secure for preservation rolls, records, books and other documents relating to that period; to encourage research and publication of historical data, including memorials of patriots of that era in our National history; to care for and, when necessary, assist in burying actual veterans of that struggle; to cherish, maintain and extend the institutions of American freedom, and foster true patriotism and love of country.

—*Courtesy of National Maritime Museum, England.*

The Baltimore County Advocate
September 16, 1860

On Sept. 12 the Old Defenders of Baltimore partook of their annual dinner on Wednesday last at Brown's Pavilion (late Houck's). The ladies connected with the Patapsco Meeting House had invited the Defenders to dine free on the battleground near the church and the invitation was accepted, but on reconsideration they canceled because it was too far from the steamboat landing at Brown's and also concluded to dine at the latter place. The church ladies thereafter prepared dinner in the grove adjoining the meeting house, and issued tickets at one dollar each, the proceeds to be applied to the repairs of the church.

HISTORY OF THE SOCIETY OF THE WAR OF 1812

[Reprinted from the Constitution and By-Laws
adopted by the Society on October 25, 1952]

A contemporary record relates that on the morning of September 14, 1814, after the repulse of the British by land and by sea, exulting citizen-soldiers from the garrisons at Fort McHenry, Port Covington, and Webster's six-gun battery at Fort Babcock, who had frustrated the British attempt to land troops in the rear of Fort McHenry, vowed that they would never thereafter disband. Historically this oath marks the birth of the Society of the War of 1812 in the State of Maryland and, through this society, of the General Society of the War of 1812.

Evidently similar sentiments were expressed by the citizen-soldiers everywhere about the embattled city; for the next year, on September 12, 1815, the anniversary of the Battle of North Point, rather than of Fort McHenry, the veterans of the defense of Baltimore met on the green, now Monument Square, where they paraded and participated in the dedication of the cornerstone of Battle Monument, to the erection of which they contributed their battle pay. The first Military Commander of the veterans was General Samuel Smith, who was succeeded in 1815 by Major-General George H. Steuart, the second Military Commander. Each year thereafter, on Defenders Day, the citizen-soldiers paraded in strength around Battle Monument, which memorializes the glory of their deeds and honors their heroic dead. In 1839 the veteran companies, together with units of the more recently organized militia, took part in the ceremonies attending the laying of the cornerstone of the Aquilla Randall monument on the battlefield at North Point.

On May 14, 1841, the veterans of the War of 1812 living in Baltimore and adjacent towns, in response to a call through the newspapers, met for the purpose of organizing a more formal veteran organization. With a complete roster of troops engaged in the defense of Baltimore in its possession, a committee selected May 14, 1842, as the day of organization of the Association of the Defenders of Baltimore in 1814. A National Encampment, attended by the surviving defenders of Baltimore, as well as troops from Virginia, Pennsylvania, and Washington, was held at Mount Clare from May 14 to May 30 of that year. The parade was reviewed by the President of the United States, Chief of Staff General Winfield Scott, and numerous other dignitaries. A contemporary record informs us that "the Association of the Defenders of Baltimore of the War of 1812 were received upon entering the camp with wild cheering, 10,000 persons being present to greet them." On Defenders Day of the same year, the Old Defenders, 200 strong, carrying their old battle flags, participated in ceremonies at the monument at North Point erected at the place where Aquilla Randall of the Mechanical Company had fallen in battle.

A constitution was adopted by the Association in 1843. It provided, among other things, for the raising by dues and fines of a fund to be used for helping defray the funeral expenses of impoverished members and the education of their children, including moral and religious instruction. For many years thereafter the Association grew in numbers, many veterans entering its ranks and deaths remaining relatively few. Each year on Defenders Day, after ceremonies at Battle Monument, the Old Defenders visited nearby cities, such as York, Philadelphia, and Washington, or celebrated with a dinner nearer home.

There coexisted at this time an Association of the Sons of the Defenders, for in 1857 a delegation from the Sons invited the Old Defenders to be their guests at a dinner. Following the enthusiastic acceptance of the invitation, a motion to admit the sons as adjunct members of the veterans Association was, after debate, referred to a committee, which the next year reported in favor of keeping the two association separate "until such time when this association shall be unable for want of members to continue its aims and purposes." Nevertheless, looking towards the future, the Association of the Defenders empowered the Sons "to do the work laid down for us in the Constitution and with amendments and alterations as they may deem necessary for the furtherance and continuance of the yearly celebration of the Anniversary of the battle of North Point, the elevation of American citizenship and to foster patriotism, to be ever as ready as their fathers were to take up arms against a common enemy in the defence of our independence." This report as adopted amounted to a constitutional change with part membership in the Association for the Sons, to be followed by full membership as veteran strength declined.

The Association with 230 local members and 46 from out of town, was then probably at its greatest strength. Each spring it held a business meeting at its headquarters in the City Hall, and each September 12 it celebrated Defenders Day at Battle Monument with a military escort of the State militia. Inevitably with the passing years the ranks of the Old Defenders were reduced to a feeble handful of survivors of those proud companies of citizen-soldiers who had saved their city from ruin and pillage. These aged few must now be driven around the Monument in carriages, and the dinner following the patriotic celebration must be held at places in or near Baltimore. At last, in February 1880, necessity dictating the decision, the first descendant, "William H. Daneker, grandson of our venerable President," was invited into the ranks of the Association and elected its Secretary and Marshal. Two descendants were noted among the thirteen members present that year at the Defenders Day ceremonies.

In the declining years of the Association of Defenders, it was the custom of Mr. Robert Rennert to entertain the surviving Old Defenders at his famous hotel. The last dinner at which a Defender member (Joseph C. Momford) was present was held on September 12, 1887. The next year, the two remaining Defenders being too enfeebled to attend, "No attempt was made at a meeting or celebration." It was in this year, by authority granted them thirty years before, that the descendants tookover the reins of the veteran organization, calling themselves the Association of the Descendants of the Defenders of Baltimore in the War of 1812. The Association [sic] was incorporated on October 25, 1893, under the title of the Society of the War of 1812 in the State of Maryland.

In 1881 a letter from Mr. Hay, Secretary of the Pennsylvania Society of the Soldiers of 1812, proposing a union of the two organizations of veterans, had received no positive action. However, on April 12, 1894, delegates from these two associations met in Philadelphia with delegates from recently-formed associations of descendants in Massachusetts and Connecticut and organized the General Society of the War of 1812.

John A. Pentz

Old Defenders' Reunion, photographed at the commemoration of the Battle of North Point, 12 September 1881, at the Druid Hill Mansion House in Baltimore. The man in the center holds a flag and the younger man, a drummer, rests upon two old style drums on the far right. The Maryland Society Archives picture.

PREFACE

This volume is arranged alphabetically by surname of the veteran of the War of 1812 for whom a member of the Maryland Society claims direct or collateral descent. A brief biographical sketch is provided of the soldiers, seamen, or marines. Each entry consists of: dates and places of birth, death, marriage, and service during the War of 1812. The name of the member(s) claiming descent is provided at the end of the entry.

The data for these biographical sketches came only from the membership application papers. As a result, some of the information is not complete. A standard format was established as illustrated below:

    ABEY, Joseph
        b. 2 Mar 1792, Lancaster Co., PA
        d. 1 Feb 1864, Baltimore, MD
        m. Sarah Ann Saffron, 16 Jul 1835, Baltimore, MD
        Service: Private, Captain Rogers' Company, 51st Rgt., Maryland Militia.
        Member - Joseph Gregory Abey [606/3748]
                      Joseph Samuel Abey [594/3560]

When the name of the spouse or date of marriage was not provided by the member this line was not included in the entry. Sometimes only the given and not the maiden name of the spouse (or vice versa) was given in the member's application. When this occurred the entry appears as follows: Sarah -- / or / -- Dykins, followed by the date and place of marriage.

With regard to the member claiming descent, following his name two numbers appear in brackets. The first is the Maryland State Society membership number and the second is the National Society's number. Should there be more than one descendant member, they are arranged alphabetically.

The name index that follows the biographical entries is only for those individuals whose surname is different from the veteran. In the above example only Sarah Ann Saffron and Captain Rogers would be indexed. If the member Joseph Gregory or Joseph Samuel had a surname different from the ancestor then they would be included in the index and their given names italicized to distinguish them from non-members.

                                                                Thomas L. Hollowak

INTRODUCTION

The establishment of a Society of the War of 1812 in Maryland during 1893 and 1894 reflected an attitude and response common in the national mentality of the period. Mounting immigration during the second half of the century concerned the ethic which valued a long heritage on this continent. From 1881 to 1900 more than nine million Europeans were naturalized: a number equal to all who entered from 1820 to 1880.

Manifesting a "native" attitude were the numerous hereditary-patriotic organizations founded in the closing years of the past century. Some of that group are: Sons of the American Revolution, 1889; Colonial Dames of America, 1890; Daughters of the American Revolution; Netherlands Society of Philadelphia, 1892; Sons of the Republic of Texas, 1893; General Society of Colonial Wars, 1893; United Daughters of the Confederacy, 1894 and Order of Founders and Patriots of America, 1896.

In June 1892 Dr. Albert Hadel of Baltimore was active in fostering a society the membership of which would combine the communality of social acquaintance and the claim to descent from a forebear who served in the War of 1812. An informal organization with a cadre of Baltimore gentleman was composed on Defenders' Day. After taking the name Association of the Descendants of the Defenders of 1812-1814, upwards of sixty members enrolled, including several veterans of the conflict. Louis Griffith, Esq. served as President. The Fall of 1893 the Association relinquished the traditional *Defenders* title, thus moving into a new mode when the Baltimore City Court granted a Charter to Mr. Griffith, Dr. Hadel and eight other incorporators with full corporate rights and responsibilities for the Society of the War of 1812 in Maryland of Baltimore City. The patent provided no benevolent conditions, but played heavily to advance the remembrance of the war, to promote fellowship among members, to inspire patriotism, to encourage research, to publication and preservation of records and to lead in the celebration of the war's anniversaries. Within six months the fledgling organization joined with several East Coast state societies in effecting a General Society of the War of 1812.

With the issuance in 1895 of the first annotated member roster, the Maryland society had taken in 120 members. A recapitulation of December 1, 1895 enumerated seven resignations and eight deaths. At that time, of the 105 remaining compatriots, all resided in the city of Baltimore with the exception of four who lived in the Maryland counties and seven in other states.

The locations of the residential and business addresses of a notable majority of the membership were in Baltimore's more affluent areas of the year 1895. Many men were of the learned professions while the largest contingent were representatives of the business and banking communities. The first 120 to join comprised twenty-nine sons, sixty-one grandsons, and fifteen great-grandsons. In addition, membership was held by four War of 1812 veterans of very advanced age. The collective *propositi*: four served in the U.S. Army, two in the U.S. Navy, three in the militia of Virginia and North Carolina. The balance were credited with service in the Maryland Militia.

The Maryland society consistently maintained a roster seldom greater than 150 members: a fulfillment addressed to the incorporator's concern for a society with a strong fellowship. After attaining an enrollment of 142 descendants in 1900, the numbers gradually declined to 97 in 1950. Since that year a slow and irregular increase has been evident, to the attainment in 1990 of 183 compatriots. If a track of the roster were shown, it would readily be obvious that national and local events correlate with the general interest in and size of the membership.

At the close of the society's first century, the membership roll approaches 190 persons. The future of this society and others like it, is open to question particularly when given the seemingly disruptive and fluid cultural and social deviations in the order of American life as a new century beckons. However, similar speculations certainly came to mind at other periods in the society's existence.

This work was initiated in 1990 during the re-archiving of the Maryland papers which had experienced a dubious tending since 1893. Retrievals were successful in numerous unthought-of locations and missing documents were necessarily reconstructed from the most reliable original source material. It became patently clear that the newly developed, more complete and more revealing picture of the society offered a trove of historical and genealogical data previously not utilizable for study and research.

One hundred years is a convenient span of time in which to frame a reference dealing with events and attitudes. Consistent with a tenet of the incorporators, the society's centennial year offers the appropriate moment to catalog and publish the biographies of more than five hundred soldiers, seamen and marines who are the *propositi* constituting the core and foundation of lineage research for the nearly eight-hundred Maryland members during the past century.

In drawing the contents for this publication, a standard was established which allowed only material possessed of factual basis and coming from primary sources. Any item or body of conjecture was excluded. The reader can immediately recognize the need for these limitations when compiling a work of this form. The preface will detail the method and usage maintained in the presentation style to the best advantage of the casual or serious peruser.

It is with gratitude to Dr. H. Mebane Turner, President of the University of Baltimore, and the staff of the University's Langsdale Library, particularly that of the Archives, who are the custodians of the Society's archival collection. It would not have been possible to add this Centennial publication to the historical record without their generous assistance.

Baltimore, Maryland   Dennis F. Blizzard

CHRONICLE OF SOLDIERS, SEAMEN, AND MARINES

A CHRONICLE OF SOLDIERS, SEAMEN, AND MARINES

ABEY, Joseph
- b. 2 Mar 1792, Lancaster Co., PA
- d. 1 Feb 1864, Baltimore, MD
- m. Sarah Ann Saffron, 16 Jul 1835, Baltimore, MD
- Service: Private, Captain Rogers' Company, 51st Rgt., Maryland Militia.
- **Member** - Joseph Gregory Abey [606/3748]
  Joseph Samuel Abey [594/3560]

ACHESON, Thomas
- b. Armagh, Ireland
- d. 1815, Washington, PA
- Service: Brigadier General, 14th Division, Pennsylvania Volunteers, 1812. Promoted to Major General in 1813.
- **Member** - Calvin Hooker Goddard [410/2180]

ADAMS, Alexander
- b. 1773, Scotland
- d. 25 Jun 1823, At Sea
- m. Cristine Beaufeau, 17 Mar 1797, Bordeaux, France
- Service: Captain, Six gun privateer - *Amelia*.
- **Member** - Isaac Wimbert Mohler, Jr. [257/1178]

ADAMS, Minos
- b. 1 May 1776, MD
- d. MD
- Service: Captain, 11th Rgt., Maryland Militia. Resigned, 25 Jan 1814.
- **Member** - Laurence Purdy Sangston (collateral) [611/3773]

AISQUITH, Edward
- b. 11 Dec 1778, Baltimore Co., MD
- d. 23 Feb 1815, Ellicott Mills, MD
- m. Sarah Lyttleton Moore, 29 Dec 1804, Charles Town, WV
- Service: Captain, Company of Sharp Shooters, 1st Rifle Battilion, Maryland Militia. 19 Aug - 18 Nov 1814.
- **Member** - Antony Joseph Trapnell Kloman [601/3691]

A CHRONICLE OF SOLDIERS, SEAMEN, AND MARINES

ALBAUGH, William
    b. 1782, Baltimore, MD
    d. Jan 1868, Baltimore, MD
    m. Elizabeth Sellers
    Service: Private, Color Bearer, Baltimore County Company, Maryland Militia.
    Member - Jacob Albaugh [57/285]

ALER, Thomas
    b. 1792, MD
    d. Oct 1862, MD
    m. Catherine French
    Service: Private, Captain Decker's Company, 7th Rgt. Maryland Militia.
    Member - Ashton Schiaffino [635/4752]
            George Evans Schiaffino [659/4199]

ALFORD, Ami
    b. 27 Jun 1791, Fenisburg, VT
    d. 25 Jun 1862, Watersville, VT
    m. Clarissa White
    Service: Private, Captain Jacks' Company, 7th Rgt., New York Artillery. 21 Sep - 30 Dec 1812.
    Member - Albert Gallatin Alford [177/944]

APPLEBY, John
    b. 1790, Montgomery Co., MD
    d. 16 Feb 1834, Baltimore, MD
    m. Elizabeth Shield
    Service: Private, Captain James Foster's Company, 51st Rgt., Maryland Militia.
    Member - Francis Barnum Culver [107/426]

APPOLD, George
    b. 4 Apr 1793, Baltimore, MD
    d. 22 Jan 1853, Baltimore, MD
    m. Elizabeth Boget, 4 Jan 1816, Baltimore, MD
    Service: Corporal in Captain Chalmer's Company, 51st Rgt., Maryland Militia.
    Member - James Frederick Adams, 4th [496/2734]

A CHRONICLE OF SOLDIERS, SEAMEN, AND MARINES

ARBAUGH (Earbaugh), John
    b. 12 Aug 1775, Upper Delaware Hundred, MD
    d. 18 Feb 1842, Westminster, MD
    m. Margaret Long, 25 Dec 1820, Baltimore Co., MD
    Service: Private, Captain William Blizzard's Company, 15th Rgt. Baltimore Co., 11th Brigade, Maryland Militia. 15 Aug 1813 - 19 Sep 1814.
    Member - Arthur Keith Blizzard [610/3839]
        Dennis Craig Blizzard [603/3696]
        Dennis Frizzell Blizzard [523/2969]

ARMISTEAD, George
    b. VA
    d. 25 Apr 1818, Baltimore, MD
    m. Louisa Hughes
    Service: Brevet Lieutenant Colonel. U.S. Army, 12 Sep 1814.
    Member - George Armistead [209/1036]

ARMSTRONG, Peter
    b. 1777, Calmar, Sweden
    d. 1 Jan 1837, Baltimore, MD
    m. Bathsheba Wood
    Service: Private, Captain Thomas Carbery's Company, 36th U.S. Infantry, stationed at Fort McHenry during the bombardment. 23 Jul 1814 - 21 Mar 1815.
    Member - Taylor Addison [56/282]

ARMSTRONG, Thomas
    b. County Tyrone, Ireland
    d. 1824, Baltimore, MD
    m. Ellen Curran
    Service: Private, Baltimore Union Artillery.
    Member - Charles Sylvester Grindall [208/1028]

ASHBY, Nimrod
    b. 7 Oct 1778, Farquier Co., VA
    d. 1 Jan 1830, Farquier Co., VA
    m. Mary Turner, Farquier Co., VA
    Service: Captain, 44th Rgt., Virginia Militia. 31 Mar - 22 Oct 1813.
    Member - Bernard Ashby [326/1531]

A CHRONICLE OF SOLDIERS, SEAMEN, AND MARINES

AUD, Asa
    b. 1783, nr. Buckeystown, MD
    d. 1860, nr. Edward's Ferry, MD
    m. Caroline Hickman, 15 Sep 1821, nr. Poolesville, MD
    Service: Sergeant, Captain Turbett's Company, 3rd Rgt., Maryland Militia.
        1 Sep - 31 Oct 1814.
    Member - Edward Trujean Aud [577/3363]

BAER, Jacob Shellman
    b. 22 May 1783, Frederick, MD
    d. 10 Apr 1866, Frederick, MD
    m. Elizabeth Worthington Dorsey, 12 Jan 1813, Anne Arundel Co., MD
    Service: Surgeon's Mate, 16th Rgt., Maryland Militia.
    Member - Herbert Lou Baer, Sr. [665/4140]

BAGBY, John
    b. 25 May 1761, Louisa Co., VA
    d. 17 Nov 1834, Barren Co., KY
    m. Matilda Davis, 20 Dec 1792, Amherst Co., VA
    Service: Captain of Cavalry, 9th Rgt., Virginia Militia. 4 Apr 1813 - 10 Dec 1814.
    Member - Henry Clint Peden, Jr. [672/4283]

BALDWIN, Justus
    b. 6 Jul 1788, Essex Co., NJ
    d. 22 Jan 1846, Newark, NJ
    Service: Private, Captain Baldwin's Company, New Jersey Militia.
        1 Sep - 7 Dec 1814.
    Member - William Brand Pryor (collateral) [585/3454]
        William Young Pryor (collateral) [556/2671]

A CHRONICLE OF SOLDIERS, SEAMEN, AND MARINES

BALDWIN, William Henry
    b. 11 Sep 1792, Anne Arundel Co., MD
    d. 6 Apr 1874, Anne Arundel Co., MD
    m. Jane Maria Woodward, 7 Oct 1817, Anne Arundel Co., MD
    Service: U.S. Navy, 1812-1814.
    Member - Charles Elliott Baldwin [447/2341]
          Charles Gambrill Baldwin [348/1632]
          John Ashby Baldwin [359/1695]
          Summerfield Baldwin, Jr. [356/1651]
          Willard Augustine Baldwin [355/1650]

BANDEL, William
    b. 1786, Germany
    d. 15 Oct 1871, Baltimore, MD
    m. Mary Clark
    Service: Private, 1st Company, 6th Rgt., Maryland Militia.
    Member - Littleton Chandler Bandel [154/764]

BARNEY, Joshua
    b. 6 Jul 1759, Baltimore, MD
    d. 1 Dec 1818, Pittsburgh, PA
    m. Anne Bedford, 16 Mar 1780
    Service: Captain, U.S. Navy, 1812-1814.
    Member - Frederic Arthur Winsor Bryan [534/3023]
          William Barney Harris [304/1490]
          William Barney Harris, Jr. [322/1526]

BARRETT, John Miller
    b. 17 Nov 1788, Baltimore, MD
    d. 16 Oct 1819, On Shipboard
    m. Mary Leahy, Jan 1812, Baltimore
    Service: Lieutenant, 38th Rgt., U.S. Infantry. 20 May 1813- May 1814.
    Member - John L. Barrett [45/229]
          John Minot Barrett [298/1461]

A CHRONICLE OF SOLDIERS, SEAMEN, AND MARINES

BARROLL, James Edmondson
    b. 24 Aug 1779, Easton, MD
    d. 24 Dec 1875, Holly Hall, MD
    m. Henrietta Jane Hackett, 15 Jun 1824, Chestertown, MD
    Service: Secretary and Adjutant of Troop of Horse, Maryland Militia.
        5 Jun 1813 - 30 Aug 1814.
    Member - David Oakley Vanderpoel Barroll [711/4705]
        Reginald Stewart Barroll [685/4490]

BAY, Thomas
    b. abt. 1789, Harford Co., MD
    d. Harford Co., MD
    Service: Private, Captain Turner's Company, 42nd Rgt., Maryland Militia.
        28 Aug - 26 Sep 1814.
    Member - Ambler Jones Stewart [192/973]

BAYLESS, Benjamin
    b. 4 Feb 1774, Harford Co., MD
    d. 13 Oct 1839, Washington Co., KY
    Service: Captain, Kentucky Militia, 31 Aug - Nov 1812.
    Member - Samuel Poyntz Cochran [366/1720]

BEALL, John
    b. 23 December 1781, Montgomery Co., MD
    d. 26 August 1831, Montgomery Co., MD
    m. Charlotte Jones, 5 Jan 1807, Montgomery Co., MD
    Service: Private, Captain Vinson's Company, 32nd Rgt., Maryland Militia.
        1 Aug 1814 - 27 Sep 1814.
    Member - Abell Archibald Norris, Jr. [541/3071]

BEALMEAR, Francis
    b. 1780, Anne Arundel Co., MD
    d. 1834, Anne Arundel Co., MD
    m. Sarah Warfield, 9 Oct 1811, Anne Arundel Co., MD
    Service: Captain, 2nd Rgt., Maryland Militia. 6 Jul 1814.
    Member - James Irving Bealmer, Jr. [525/2980]

A CHRONICLE OF SOLDIERS, SEAMEN, AND MARINES

BEARD, John
    b. 19 Oct 1790, Anne Arundel Co., MD
    d. 12 May 1857, Baltimore, MD
    m. Martha Lambert
    Service: Sergeant, Captain Schwarzaner's Company, 27th Rgt., Maryland Militia.
    Member - Benjamin Harrison Waring [173/933]

BEATTY, Henry
    b. 23 Sep 1760, Frederick, MD
    d. 23 Apr 1840, Winchester, VA
    m. Sarah Henning, 30 Sep 1783, Culpepper, VA
    Service: Lieutenant Colonel, 4th Battalion, Virginia Militia. 22 Jun 1813.
    Member - John Overington [600/3633]
            Robert Bruce Overington [401/2072]

BEERS, Abel
    b. 19 Jan 1790, Fairfield, CT
    d. 10 Mar 1874, Fairfield, CT
    m. Elizabeth Whitney, 24 Dec 1808, Fairfield, CT
    Service: Private, Captain Sherwood's Detachment, 4th Rgt., Connecticut Militia. 15 - 17 Apr 1814.
    Member - Walter Whitney Beers [345/1624]

BEETEM, Abraham
    b. 27 Aug 1789, Berks Co., PA
    d. 12 Aug 1833, Huntsdale, PA
    m. Elizabeth Smith, 15 Nov 1815, Lancaster Co., PA
    Service: Captain, 59th Rgt., Pennsylvania Milita.
    Member - Donald Gilbert Beetem [592/3550]
            Edward Charles Beetem [505/2793]
            Douglas Howard Everngam [696/4501]
            George Gregg Everngam [595/3565]

A CHRONICLE OF SOLDIERS, SEAMEN, AND MARINES

BELL, Cecelius
    b. 2 Mar 1792, Baltimore Co., MD
    d. 12 Sep 1814, Battle of North Point
    Service: Private, Captain Haubert's Company, 51st Rgt., Maryland Militia.
        7 - 12 Sep 1814.
    Member - Arthur Clifton Bushey, Jr. (collateral) [559/3186]

BELOTE, Charles
    b. 1785, Accomac, VA
    d. 1843, Accomac, VA
    m. Elizabeth Martin
    Service: Private, Captain Scarborough's Company, 2nd Rgt., Virginia Militia.
        5 Apr 1814 - 8 Oct 1818.
    Member - Adelbert Warren Mears [350/1636]
        Christian Emmerich Mears [351/1637]

BENNETT, Archibald
    b. 12 Jan 1763, Washington Co., MD
    d. 1841, Decatur Co., IL
    m. Martha Duvall, 24 Jul 1790, Maysville, KY
    Service: 25th U.S. Infantry. 8 Aug 1812 - 28 Feb 1814.
    Member - Paul Warren Bennett [618/3849]

BERRY, John
    b. 2 Nov 1791, Prince Georges Co., MD
    d. 17 Oct 1856, Baltimore Co., MD
    m. Sarah D. Jackson
    Service: Captain, Washington Artillery, 1st Rgt. attached to 34th Brigade, Maryland
        Militia.
    Member - Robert Berry Bull [129/608]
        Lyteleton Bowen Purcell Gould [389/1885]
        John Hurst Morgan [106/425]
        Philip Sidney Morgan [383/1826]

A CHRONICLE OF SOLDIERS, SEAMEN, AND MARINES

BIAYS, James
    b. 25 May 1791, Baltimore, MD
    d. 28 Sep 1865, Washinton Co., MD
    m. Margareth McMullins, 23 Dec 1817, Philadelphia, PA
    Service: Lieutenant Colonel, 5th Rgt. Cavalry, Maryland Militia.
        19 Aug - 18 Oct 1814.
    Member - James Philip Biays [294/1437]
        Tolley Allender Biays [249/1157]
        John Barry Mahool [194/980]

BIRCKHEAD, Hugh
    b. 6 Sep 1788, Cambridge, MD
    d. 22 Jan 1853, Baltimore, MD
    m. Catherine Augustas McEvers
    Service: Private, Independent Company, 5th Rgt., Maryland Militia.
    Member - Lennox Birckhead [143/695]

BISBEE, Daniel
    b. 7 May 1791, Sumner, ME
    d. 24 Apr 1824, Sumner, ME
    m. Sylvia Stephens, 1 Jan 1815, Sumner, ME
    Service: In Lieutenant Stevens' Company, Maine Militia.
    Member - Horace Kimball Richardson [475/2603]

BISSELL, Daniel Russell
    b. 30 Jul 1769, Windsor, CT
    d. 15 Dec 1833, St. Louis, MI
    m. Deborah Saborn
    Service: Colonel, U.S. Army, 15 Aug 1812. Brevet Brigadier General, 20 Apr 1815.
    Member - Brian Wesley Brooke [615/3832]
        Dandridge Brooke [625/3967]
        Dandridge William Brooke [726/4816]
        Randall Whitney Brooke [626/3968]

A CHRONICLE OF SOLDIERS, SEAMEN, AND MARINES

BIXLER, David
    b. 26 Oct 1775, Carroll Co., MD
    d. 11 Oct 1832, Baltimore, MD
    m. Mary Magdalene Utz, 2 Nov 1803, Carroll Co., MD
    Service: Private, 1st Baltimore Artillery, Maryland Militia.
    Member - William Henry Harrison Bixler [273/1303]

BLACK, Noah
    b. 4 Sep 1791, Caroline Co., MD
    d. 19 Oct 1856, Caroline Co., MD
    m. Margaret Keets, 1 May 1814, Caroline Co., MD
    Service: (Suspended Bounty Claim #235976)
    Member - Ronald Milton Finch [620/3881]
        Willard Robert Finch [663/4203]

BLACKLOCK, Nicholas Frederick, II
    b. 1791, Prince Georges Co., MD
    d. 1818, Alexandria, Washington, D.C.
    m. Elizabeth Johnson Ramsay
    Service: First Lieutenant, Captain McElderry's Detachment, 17th Rgt., Maryland Militia. 18 Jun - 13 Sep 1814.
    Member - Aubrey Henry Blacklock, Jr. [536/3030]

BLIZZARD, William of W.
    b. 1774, Baltimore Co., MD
    d. 13 Nov 1816, Westminster, MD
    m. Ruth Taylor, 19 May 1802, Baltimore Co., MD
    Service: Captain, 15th Rgt., 11th Brigade, Maryland Militia. 13 Aug 1813 - 19 Sep 1814.
    Member - Arthur Keith Blizzard [610/3839]
        Dennis Craig Blizzard [603/3696]
        Dennis Frizzell Blizzard [523/2969]

A CHRONICLE OF SOLDIERS, SEAMEN, AND MARINES

BLOOMER, Daniel
    b. Hunter Green Co., NY
    d. 1855, Huron Co., OH
    m. Johana Haines
    Service: Private, Captain Belknap's Company, 2nd Rgt., New York Militia.
        18 Aug - 2 Dec 1814.
    Member - Alfred Elliott Sharp [254/1175]
        Alfred Elliott Sharp, Jr. [370/1727]

BLUNT, Francis
    b. 21 Oct 1776, Hanover Co., VA
    d. 9 Aug 1851, Hanover Co., VA
    m. Elizabeth Dodswell Harris, 31 Jan 1811, VA
    Service: Captain in Virginia Militia.
    Member - Guy Hudson Parr, Jr. [460/2552]
        Lee Sutherland Parr [439/2317]

BOBART, Charles Carroll
    b. abt. 1789, Kent Co., MD
    d. 17 Mar 1869, Baltimore, MD
    m. Charlotte Swift
    Service: 1st Corporal, 5th Company, 6th Rgt., Maryland Militia.
    Member - Charles Carroll Bobart [100/403]

BOBST, Daniel
    b. 1796, PA
    d. 15 Feb 1840, Frederick, MD
    m. Mary Shuck, 8 Sep 1818, Frederick, MD
    Service: Private, Captain Turnbull's Company, 1st Rgt., Maryland Militia.
        2 Sept - 6 Nov 1814.
    Member - Charles Edward Kemp [708/4707]

BOGGS, Alexander Lowry
    b. 13 Oct 1792, Lancaster Co., PA
    d. 12 Aug 1856, Baltimore, MD
    m. Susan Greer
    Service: Private, 1st Baltimore Hussars, 5th Rgt., Maryland Militia.
    Member - Francis Henry Boggs [85/388]

A CHRONICLE OF SOLDIERS, SEAMEN, AND MARINES

BOLLMAN, Thomas Gottlieb
    b. 18 May 1775, Breman, Germany
    d. 19 Jan 1866, Baltimore, MD
    m. Ann Barbara Raab, 15 Apr 1805, Baltimore, MD
    Service: Corporal, Captain Steever's Company, 27th Rgt., Maryland Militia.
        9 Aug - 16 Aug 1813. Private, Captain Kane's Company, 27th Rgt., Maryland Militia. 19 Aug - 18 Nov 1814.
    Member - William Wendell Bollman McKinnell [344/1607]

BOND, Thomas E.
    b.
    d. 1855, Baltimore, MD
    m. Christiana Birckhead
    Service: Surgeon, 7th Rgt., Maryland Militia.
    Member - Thomas Murray Maynadier [217/1054]

BOND, Thomas Talbott
    b. 14 Aug 1792, Harford Co., MD
    d. 21 Mar 1875, White House, MD
    m. Mary Ann --, 21 Nov 1821, Harford Co., MD
    Service: Private, Captain Warfield's Company, Baltimore United Volunteers, Maryland Militia. 10 Mar - 12 Sep 1814.
    Member - Calhoun Bond [687/4491]

BORDEN, Francis
    b. 20 Mar 1780, Shrewsbury, NJ
    d. Shrewsbury, NJ
    m. Mary Erwin, 18--, Shrewsbury Friends Meeting House, NJ
    Service: Captain, 3rd Rgt., Monmouth Brigade, New Jersey Militia.
        Spring 1814 to close of the War.
    Member - Peter Lloyd Woolsey Brathwaite [570/3276]
        William Henry Lloyd [396/1960]
        Edward Parker Street [578/3388]

A CHRONICLE OF SOLDIERS, SEAMEN, AND MARINES

BOSWELL, Henry
    b. 2 Jan 1791, Charles Co., MD
    d. 22 Sep 1882, Ohio Co., KY
    Service: Private, Lieutenant Gardiner's Detachment, 1st Rgt., Maryland Militia.
        24 Jul - 24 Aug 1814.
    Member - Frederick Page Boswell [376/1767]

BOULDEN, Nathaniel L.
    b. 3 May 1781, Cecil Co., MD
    d. 5 Feb 1835, Cecil Co., MD
    m. Rebecca Dean, 9 Jan 1803, Cecil Co., MD
    Service: Surgeon's Mate (later Surgeon), U.S. Infantry. 3 Jul 1813 - 15 Jun 1815.
    Member - Charles Newton Boulden [292/1429]

BOULDIN, Jehu
    b. 1760, Baltimore, MD
    d. 5 May 1830, Baltimore, MD
    m. Mary Askew, 16 May 1794, Baltimore, MD
    Service: Captain, Independent Light Dragoons, 5th Rgt., Maryland Militia.
    Member - Augustus Bouldin [58/288]
        Thomas Stevens George [444/2339]
        Thomas Stevens George, Jr. [555/3163]

BOWE, Nathaniel
    b. 1765, Hanover Co., VA
    d. 1829, Hanover Co., VA
    m. Susannah Davis, 1788, Hanover Co., VA
    Service: Captain, 74th Rgt. Virginia Militia.
    Member - Dudley Pleasants Bowe [518/2939]

BRAMBLE, Moses
    b. 1790
    d. 11 Aug 1844, Bishops Head, MD
    m. Elizabeth Rumbley, 11 Nov 1814, Dorchester Co., MD
    Service: Private, Captain Jones' Company, 48th Rgt., Maryland Militia.
        1813 - 1814.
    Member - Carroll Jefferson Collins [720/4793]

A CHRONICLE OF SOLDIERS, SEAMEN, AND MARINES

BRANDEBERRY, Philip
    b. 1786, Westmoreland Co., PA
    d. Jan 1867, Perry Township, OH
    m. Catharine Zimmerman, before 1812
    Service: Corporal & Sergeant, 4th Rgt., 20th Brigade, Ohio Militia.
        Aug 1812 - Feb 1813.
    Member - Winfield Ross Smith [529/2984]

BRICE, Nicholas
    b. 23 Apr 1771, Annapolis, MD
    d. 9 May 1851, Baltimore, MD
    m. Anna Maria Tilghman, Chestertown, MD
    Service: Private, Captain Sterret's Independent Company, 5th Rgt., Maryland Militia.
        19 Aug - 18 Nov 1814.
    Member - Carroll Allyn Brice [513/2857]
        A. Weems McFadden [661/4201]

BRISTOR, George
    b. 1791, VA
    d. 30 May 1826, Baltimore, MD
    m. Susan Lusby, 27 Jul 1820, Baltimore, MD
    Service: Private, Virginia Militia. 15 May - 15 Jun 1814.
    Member - Joseph Whitridge Bristor [248/1156]
        William Beverly Bristor [291/1426]
        William Beverly Bristor, Jr. [572/3279]

BROHAWN, John
    b. Apr 1761, Dorchester Co., MD
    d. 10 Nov 1820, Dorchester Co., MD
    Service: Captain, 48th Rgt., Maryland Militia.
    Member - Stuart Cator Hooper [392/1889]

BROMLEY, Lewis
    b. 6 Aug 1787, VT
    d. 29 Jan 1834, Baltimore, MD
    m. Ann Catherine Irons, 26 Dec 1819, Baltimore, MD
    Service: Sergeant, 38th Rgt., U.S. Infantry
    Member - John Lewis Bromley [144/711]

A CHRONICLE OF SOLDIERS, SEAMEN, AND MARINES

BROWN, Eli
    b. 1767, MA
    d. Aug 1820, Amherst, NH
    m. Sarah Hopkins
    Service: Sailing Master, U.S. Navy. 25 April 1812 - 13 Sep 1814.
    Member - Archibald George William McFadden [717/4769]

BROWN, John
    b. 1798, Baltimore, MD
    d. 7 Mar 1865, Baltimore, MD
    m. Mary Allen, 13 Jun 1816, Baltimore, MD
    Service: Private in Captain Rogers' Company, 51st Rgt., Maryland Militia.
        3 Sep 1814 - 22 Sep 1814.
    Member - John Prentiss Brown [728/4818]

BRUCE, Robert
    b. Scotland
    d. Baltimore, MD
    m. Anne Schoffield, 8 Jan 1807, Baltimore, MD
    Service: In Captain Roney's Company, 39th Rgt., Maryland Militia.
    Member - Oliver Herman Bruce [258/1179]

BRUMFIELD, William
    b. 27 Nov 1776, Port Deposit, MD
    d. 4 Mar 1841, Port Deposit, MD
    m. Ameilia Owens
    Service: Private, Captain Porter's Detachment, 30th Rgt., Maryland Militia.
        Apr 24-27, 1813. Private, Captain Garry's Company, 49th Rgt., Maryland
        Militia. Aug - Oct 1814.
    Member - Jerome Edgar Brumfield [225/1074]

A CHRONICLE OF SOLDIERS, SEAMEN, AND MARINES

BUCK, Benjamin
    b. abt. 1776, Baltimore Co., MD
    d. 28 Oct 1848, Baltimore, MD
    m. Catherine Reese
    Service: 1st Lieutenant, Washington Artillery, 1st Rgt., Maryland Militia.
    Member - George Hickman Buck [135/662]
        Edward Burneston Owens [138/687]
        Edward Burneston Owens, Jr. [333/1588]
        Frederick Charles Peregoy [418/2237]
        Robert Lee Porter, Jr. [357/1666]

BUCK, Benjamin
    b. 18 Dec 1795, Baltimore Co., MD
    d. 1841, Baltimore Co., MD
    m. Jane Herbert, 16 Aug 1820, Baltimore, MD
    Service: Cornet, Captain Stansbury's Company, 6th Calvary District, Maryland
        Militia. 14 Jul 1812.
    Member - Herbert Lee Trueheart [453/2347]

BUCK, William Richardson
    b. 4 Aug 1790, VA
    d. 9 Oct 1853, LA
    m. Maria Flower Dalton, 29 Jan 1822, West Feliciana Parish, LA
    Service: Midshipman, U.S. Navy. 1 Jan 1812 - 25 Jan 1815.
    Member - Edward Harvey Brinton [517/2911]

BUCKINGHAM, Levi
    b. 18 Jul 1786, Baltimore, MD
    d. 14 Apr 1831, Baltimore, MD
    m. Elizabeth Cole
    Service: Private, Captain Blizzard's Company, 15th Rgt., Maryland Militia.
    Member - Charles Wesley Buckingham [28/188]

A CHRONICLE OF SOLDIERS, SEAMEN, AND MARINES

BUNTING, John
- b. 1782, Harford Co., MD
- d. 1847 St. Joseph, MI
- m. Mary Sommerville
- Service: Private, Captain Michael Peter's Company, 51st Rgt., Maryland Militia.
- **Member** - Thomas Ireland Elliott [118/507]

BURGOON, Jacob
- b. 28 Aug 1788, Taneytown, MD
- d. 9 Dec 1874, Somerset, OH
- Service: Private in Captain Foustiens Company, Maryland Militia. 2 Sep - 28 Oct 1814.
- **Member** - Norman Aaron Burgoon, Jr. (collateral) [565/3208]

BURNESTON, William Reed
- b. 29 May 1797, Baltimore Co., MD
- d. 23 Jan 1871, Baltimore Co., MD
- m. Anne Rutter
- Service: Lieutenant, Captain Watts Company, 36th Rgt., 11th Brigade, Maryland Militia. 12 Oct 1814.
- **Member** - Fred Norman Newcomb [646/4079]
  Samuel Albert Rittenhouse [616/3833]

BURNS, James
- b. abt. 1785, Scotland
- d. abt. 1814, Baltimore
- m. Mary Castle
- Service: Private, Captain McConkey's Company, 27th Rgt., Maryland Militia. 19 Aug - 18 Nov 1814.
- **Member** - Douglass H. Hargett [148/734]

CADWALADER, Thomas
- b. 29 Oct 1779, Philadelphia, PA
- d. 26 Oct 1841, Philadelphia, PA
- m. Mary Biddle, 25 Jun 1804, Philadelphia, PA
- Service: Brigadier General, in command of the 4th U.S. Military District, Advance Light Brigade, Pennsylvania Volunteers.
- **Member** - Thomas Francis Cadwalader [267/1227]

A CHRONICLE OF SOLDIERS, SEAMEN, AND MARINES

CAIN, Mathew
    b. 1781, Harford Co., MD
    d. 11 Mar 1859, Harford Co., MD
    m. Sarah T. Neagle, Harford Co., MD
    Service: Cornet, Captain Macatee's Company, 7th Troop of Calvary, Maryland Militia. 16 Apr 1812.
    Member - William John Wells, Jr. [574/3283]

CALHOUN, Adam, Jr.
    b. 1778, Prince Edward Co., VA
    d. 1834, Prince Edward Co., VA
    m. Violet Davis, Prince Edward Co., VA
    Service: Captain of Prince Edward Company, Virginia Militia. 1812 - 1813.
    Member - Ernest Clyde Calhoun, Jr. [714/4766]

CAPLES, Jacob
    b. circa 1773/74, Baltimore Co., MD
    d. 6 Apr 1839, Caples Habitation, MD
    m. Mary Bassett, 27 Mar 1816, Baltimore Co., MD
    Service: Lieutenant, Captain Stephen Gill's Company, 41st Rgt., Maryland Militia.
    Member - Robert Martin Caples [640/4002]

CARROLL, William
    b. 3 Mar 1788, Wilkinsburg, PA
    d. 22 Mar 1844, Nashville, TN
    m. Cecelia Bradford, 1 Sep 1813, Sumner Co., TN
    Service: Brigade Inspector with the rank of Captain and later Major of Jackson's Division, Tennessee Volunteers, 10 Dec 1812 - 27 Apr 1813. Inspector General, Jackson's Division, Tennessee Volunteers, 26 Sep 1813 - 24/24 Jun 1814. Major General, Carroll's Division, Tennessee Militia. 13 Nov 1814 - 13 May 1815.
    Member - Luke William Finley [650/4083]

A CHRONICLE OF SOLDIERS, SEAMEN, AND MARINES

CASSARD, Gilbert
    b. 31 Dec 1781, Nantes, France
    d. 16 Nov 1857, Baltimore, MD
    Service: Private, Washington Artillery, 1st Rgt., Maryland Militia.
    Member - Jesse L. Cassard [63/297]
        John Cassard [200/1009]
        William L. Cassard [59/289]
        Edward Burneston Owens, Jr. [333/1588]
        Howard Hopkins Reese [216/1053]

CATHCART (Kithcart), Robert
    b. 1786, Baltimore, MD
    d. 24 Sep 1814, Baltimore, MD
    m. Anne Maxwell, 6 May 1813, Baltimore, MD
    Service: Private, 51st Rgt., Maryland Militia.
    Member - Asbury Roszel Cathcart [204/1023]
        Roszel Cathcart Thomsen [310/1498]

CHAMBERLAIN, Henry
    b. 1781, MD
    d. Washington, D.C.
    m. Elizabeth --
    Service: Private, Captain John's Company, District of Columbia Militia.
        20 May - 19 Aug 1813.
    Member - Herbert Thomas Brown, Jr. [648/4081]

CHAMBERS, John McLaughlin
    b. 1790, Baltimore, MD
    d. 1838, MA
    m. Matilda Waite
    Service: Private, Baltimore Union Artillery, Maryland Militia.
    Member - Robert Marion Chambers [18/179]

A CHRONICLE OF SOLDIERS, SEAMEN, AND MARINES

CHATTLE, Thomas
   b. 1782, Gilmantown, NH
   d. 1824, Long Branch, NJ
   m. Nancy Pike, 11 Jul 1779
   Service: Physician and Surgeon in the War of 1812.
   Member - Henry Powell Hopkins [454/2354]
      Henry Powell Hopkins, Jr. [455/2355]

CHAYTOR, Daniel
   b. 26 Dec 1783, Baltimore, MD
   d. 29 Jun 1830, Baltimore, MD
   m. Sarah Sewell, 4 Mar 1813, Baltimore, MD
   Service: Captain of Marque Schooners. 13 Aug 1812 - 22 Nov 1813.
   Member - James Graham Marston [490/2730]

CHERBONNIER, Pierre
   b. 31 Mar 1781, Marenne, France
   d. 5 Apr 1866, Baltimore, MD
   m. Sarah Slorripe
   Service: Private, Captain Simpson's Company, Louisiana Militia.
      16 Dec 1814 - 28 Feb 1815.
   Member - Andrew Victor Cherbonnier [220/1057]

CHRISTHILF, Heinrich
   b. 1787, Philadelphia, PA
   d. 24 Nov 1866, Baltimore, MD
   m. Rachel Daker, 29 May 1817, Baltimore, MD
   Service: Private, Captain Henry Myers'Company, 39th Rgt., Maryland Militia.
      19 Aug - 18 Nov 1814.
   Member - Edward I. Christhilf [8/172]
      Nicholas Dorsey Christhilf [658/4198]
      Philip Raab Christhilf [660/4200]
      Stuart MacDonald Christhilf, Jr. [435/2306]
      Stuart MacDonald Christhilf, Sr. [448/2342]

A CHRONICLE OF SOLDIERS, SEAMEN, AND MARINES

CLAGETT, Elie
    b. 1781, Baltimore, MD
    d. 17 Aug 1848, Baltimore, MD
    m. Mary --, Baltimore, MD
    Service: Private, Captain Warfield's Company, Baltimore United Volunteers. Wounded at the Battle of North Point, 12 Sep 1814.
    Member - Henry Slothower [323/1527]

CLARK, Christopher
    b.
    d.
    m. Elizabeth Hock
    Service: Private, 61st Rgt., Virginia Militia. 23 Sep 1813 - 1 Mar 1815.
    Member - John Burford Hendrick, Jr. [252/1166]

CLAYTON, Philip
    b. 1780, Culpepper Co., VA
    d. 22 Jun 1863, Annapolis, MD
    Service: Corporal, Captain Slicer's Company, 22nd Rgt., Maryland Militia. 9 Apr 1813 - 16 Nov 1814.
    Member - John Philip Hill [367/1724]

CLEMENTS, Reuben
    b. Dinwiddee, VA
    d. 6 Oct 1881, Petersburg, VA
    m. Virginia Minetree
    Service: Corporal, Captain McRae's Company, Independent Volunteers, Virgina Militia.
    Member - Alfred Vernon Wall [153/754]

A CHRONICLE OF SOLDIERS, SEAMEN, AND MARINES

CLEMENTS, Thomas
    b. 15 Aug 1792, Amherst City, VA
    d. 17 Apr 1861, Paoili, IN
    m. Anne Montgomery, 14 Oct 1816, Garrard City, KY
    Service: Private, Captain William Woods' Company, 15th Rgt., Kentucky Militia.
        10 Mar - 10 May 1815.
    Member - James Stanley Clements [637/4003]

COBB, Josiah
    b. 5 Jan 1796, MA
    d. 5 Sep 1875, Baltimore, MD
    m. Amelia Jane Foster
    Service: Private, Captain J.B. Martens' Company, Massachusetts Militia.
        1 Jul - 14 Oct 1814.
    Member - Charles A. Cobb [92/396]

COCKRILL, Thomas
    b. 1769, Scotland
    d. 1 Oct 1816, Baltimore, MD
    m. Rebecca Veazy, 22 Mar 1810, Baltimore, MD
    Service: Lieutenant, Captain George J. Brown's Company, Maryland Militia.
    Member - William Calvin Chesnut Barnes [528/2983]
        Wilson King Barnes, Jr. [547/3092]

COFFMAN, Joseph [73/323]
    b. 1803
    d. 13 Feb 1897
    Service: Private and Drummer, 7th U.S. Light Infantry, Battle of New Orleans.
        8 Jan 1815.

COLE, James Alex
    b. 3 Oct 1782, Middlesex Co., England
    d. 24 Feb 1822, Baltimore, MD
    m. Charlotte McCoy
    Service: Private, Captain Wilson's Company, 6th Rgt., Maryland Militia.
    Member - John Edwin Beatty [197/997]

A CHRONICLE OF SOLDIERS, SEAMEN, AND MARINES

COLE, William
    b. Dec 1784, Cecil Co., MD
    d. 14 Aug 1844, Baltimore, MD
    m. Cassandra Smallwood
    Service: Private, 10th Company, 6th Rgt., Maryland Militia.
    Member - Robert Clinton Cole [97/401]

COLE, William
    b. 12 May 1791
    d. 13 Mar 1868, Baltimore, MD
    m. Elizabeth Clarke, 21 Jan 1813, Baltimore, MD
    Service: Defender of Baltimore, 1814.
    Member - Samuel Lyles Freeland [634/3988]

COLEMAN, Richard
    b. 1775
    d. Feb 1855, Baltimore, MD
    m. Sarah Griffin, 26 Apr 1801, Kent Co., MD
    Service: Private, Captain Gerrard Wilson's Company, 6th Rgt., Maryland Militia.
        19 Aug - 18 Nov 1814
    Member - David Coleman Watson [538/3064]

COLLINS, John Alexander
    b. England
    d. 1849, Faixfax Co., OH
    Service: Captain of Company, 1st Rgt., Ohio Militia. 21 Jul - 14 Aug 1813.
    Member - George Gordon Collins [295/1454]

COLLINS, Thomas B.
    b. circa 1795
    d. before 1850
    m. Susanna Clarke, 2 Apr 1828, Baltimore Co., MD
    Service: First Corporal, Volunteer Artillery Company, Small's Rgt., Maryland Militia.
    Member - Charles Joseph Wells [731/4857]

A CHRONICLE OF SOLDIERS, SEAMEN, AND MARINES

COLLMUS, Levi
    b. 15 Jun 1786, Prague, Bohemia
    d. 30 Mar 1856, Baltimore, MD
    m. Frances Williams, 1812, Baltimore, MD
    Service: Private, Captain Piper's Company, 1st Rgt., Maryland Militia. 19 Aug 30 Nov 1814.
    Member - Charles Carroll Collmus [234/1129]
        Clarence Richard Evans [269/1244]

CONRAD, David
    b. 23 Apr 1793, Loudoun Co., VA
    d. 14 Mar 1863, Fairfax Co., VA
    m. Sarah Ellis Thomas
    Service: Ensign, 20th U.S. Infantry, 20 July 1814. He was on recruiting service from October 1814 until he resigned December 31, 1814.
    Member - James Madison Monroe Conrad [87/389]
        Townsend Nelson Conrad [116/463]

CONTEE, John
    b. Prince George's Co., MD
    d. Laurel, MD
    Service: Lieutenant, U.S. Marine Corps, U.S. Frigate Constitution. 17 April 1812 - 15 Sep 1815.
    Member - Richard Contee [42/217]

COOK, Bernard Henry
    b. circa 1777, Philadelphia, PA
    d. 1819, Lost at Sea
    m. Anne --, 1804, Philadelphia, PA
    Service: Quartermaster and 2nd Lieutenant, 46th Rgt. 25 Jul - 1 Dec 1814.
    Member - Edwin Bernard Green [432/2302]
        Edwin Bernard Green, Jr. [499/2766]
        Richard Ellwood Green [533/3025]

A CHRONICLE OF SOLDIERS, SEAMEN, AND MARINES

COOPER, James
    b. 20 Apr 1792, Brunswick, NY
    d. 14 Apr 1872, Middlesex, NY
    m. Rebecca Wemple, 18 Mar 1827, Waterloo, NY
    Service: Private, 12th Rgt. of Calvalry (Boughton's), New York Militia.
        27 Feb - 31 Mar 1814.
    Member - Edward Franklin Cooper [702/4633]

COOPER, Robert
    b. Scotland
    d. Dec 1817, Baltimore, MD
    m. Elizabeth Railley
    Service: Sergeant, Captain William Browns Company, 6th Rgt., Maryland Militia.
    Member - Alexander Cooper Freeburger [13/8]

CRADDICK, Joseph
    b. 1778, MD
    d. 1849, Baltimore, MD
    m. Marie --
    Service: Private, 8th Company, 27th Rgt., Maryland Militia.
    Member - Joseph N. Craddick [78/364]

CRAIN, John
    b. Northumberland Co., VA (?)
    d. 1829, Fauquier Co., VA
    m. Mary Bailey
    Service: Private, Captain Nicholas Osburn's Company, Mounted Infantry.
        24 Aug - 8 Sep 1814.
    Member - Robert Leven Luckett [543/3085]

CRANE, Elias B.
    b. 17 Dec 1789, Montclair, NJ
    d. NJ
    Service: Corporal, Captain Pierson's Company, New Jersey Militia.
        1 Sep - 7 Dec 1814.
    Member - William Herbert Crane [302/1488]

A CHRONICLE OF SOLDIERS, SEAMEN, AND MARINES

CREY, Frederick
    b. 1 Jan 1778, Cologne, Germany
    d. Baltimore, MD
    m. Margaret --
    Service: Private, Baltimore Yeagars, 5th Rgt., Maryland Militia.
    Member - Frederick Crey Tarr [193/979]

CRITTENDEN, William Gatewood
    b. Sep 1787, Essex Co., VA
    d. 30 Jan 1830, Essex Co., Va
    m. Polly Thomas, abt 25 Nov 1809, Essex Co., VA
    Service: Private, Captain Evans' Troop of Cavalry, 6th Rgt., Virginia Militia.
    Member - William Lafayette Crittenden [266/1226]
        William Samuel Crittenden Walker [272/1267]

CROMWELL, Oliver
    b. 6 Mar 1787, Baltimore, MD
    d. 28 Sep 1862, Baltimore Co., MD
    m. Ellen Cromwell, 20 May 1812
    Service: Private, Captain Kelly's Company, 36th Rgt., Maryland Militia. 29 Aug - 27 Oct 1814.
    Member - Andrew Grant Comwell [311/1499]
        Benjamin Franklin Cromwell [275/1315]
        Oliver Colbert Cromwell [381/1818]

CUMMING, Robert
    b. 1754, Frederick County, MD
    d. 14 November 1825, Libertytown, MD
    m. Margaret Allen Coates, 1778
    Service: Major General, 2nd Division, Maryland Militia.
    Member - Brinson Cumming Tucker [423/2266]

CUMMINS, John
    b. 1777, Smyrna, DE
    d. 1833, Smyrna, DE
    Service: Brigadier Major, 2nd Brigade, Delaware Militia.
    Member - Lee Cummins Carey [397/1984]

A CHRONICLE OF SOLDIERS, SEAMEN, AND MARINES

CURL, Jarrott [66/307]
   b. 1796
   d. 12 Mar 1894, Baltimore, MD
   Service: Sergeant, 2nd Rgt., Mounted Volunteers. Battle of New Orleans, LA.
      23 Dec 1814 - 8 Jan 1815.

DAMES, Augustus
   b. 8 Jan 1778, Potsdam, Prussia
   d. 1 Feb 1859, Baltimore Co., MD
   m. Dianna Bungus, Baltimore Co., MD
   Service: Private, Captain Dominick Bader's Company, 1st Rifle Battalion,
      Maryland Militia. 19 Aug - 18 Nov 1814.
   Member - Daniel Edward Shehan [431/2301]
      J. Brooke Shehan [472/2598]
      Robert James Shehan [521/2967]
      William Henry Shehan [473/2599]
      William Henry Shehan, Jr. [478/2625]

DANEKER, John Jacob
   b. 4 Mar 1798, Baltimore, MD
   d. 9 Aug 1882, Baltimore, MD
   m. Ann Jarvis
   Service: Private, 7th Company, 27 Rgt., Maryland Militia. Battle of North Point, 12
      Sep 1814.
   Member - Thomas Reese Cornelius [307/1494]
      Edwin Thomas Daneker [77/363]
      William H. Daneker [A-0/156]

DANT, William
   b. 28 May 1791, Port Tobacco, MD
   d. 8 Jun 1855, Washington, D.C.
   m. Susan Fenwick, 5 Apr 1814, Washington, D.C.
   Service: In Captain Edward Edmonston's Co., District of Columbia Militia.
      15-26 Jul 1813. Captain John J. Stull's Company of Rifleman, 1st Rgt.,
      District of Columbia Militia. 19 Aug - 18 Oct 1814.
   Member - Arthur Pierce Middleton [694/4497]

A CHRONICLE OF SOLDIERS, SEAMEN, AND MARINES

DARLING, James
    b.
    d.
    Service: 3rd Corporal, 2nd Company, 51st Rgt., Maryland Militia.
    Member - Thomas G. Ford [43/218]

DASHIELL, Henry
    b. 9 Feb 1769, Somerset Co., MD
    d. 4 Oct 1830, Baltimore, MD
    m. Mary Leeke, 24 Jan 1799
    Sevice: Private, Marine Artillery, Maryland Militia.
    Member - Nicholas Leeke Dashiell [162/854]

DAUGHERTY, Daniel
    b. 1792, Beaver Co., PA
    d. 16 Apr 1874, Beaver Co., PA
    m. Elizabeth Black, Beaver Co., PA
    Service: Captain Henry's Company, 3rd Rgt., 2nd Brigade, Pennsylvania Militia. 12 Jan - 21 Mar 1814.
    Member - Samuel Edward Green, 3rd [293/1430]

DAVIDSON, James
    b. 5 Nov 1760, England
    d. 28 Nov 1841, Anne Arundel Co., MD
    m. Ameilia Reid
    Service: Private, Baltimore Union Artillery, Maryland Militia.
    Member - James Davidson Iglehart [91/395]

DAVIE, Samuel
    b. 14 Feb 1794, NY
    d. 20 Apr 1875, Bolivar, NY
    m. Jane Sism, Fall 1814, Cherry Valley, NY
    Service: Private, Captain Peter Magheris' Company, New York Militia. Captain, 1st Volunteers, Light Infantry, New York Militia. 8 Sep 1812 - 15 Nov 1814.
    Member - Daniel J. Earnshaw [671/4282]

A CHRONICLE OF SOLDIERS, SEAMEN, AND MARINES

DAVIS, Richard
    b. 20 Mar 1786, Anne Arundel Co., MD
    d. 28 Feb 1872, Howard Co., MD
    m. Rebecca Black, 28 May 1866, Baltimore Co., MD
    Service: Private, 22nd Rgt., Maryland Militia. 28 Jul - 1 Sep 1813.
    Member - William Thomas Davis, Jr. [744/4962]

DAVY, Hugh
    b. 1776, Baltimore, MD
    d. 19 Aug 1849, Baltimore, MD
    m. Elizabeth --
    Service: Private, Marine Artillery, Maryland Militia.
    Member - Charles W. Nash [41/216]

De La ROCHE, George Henri Frederick Franck
    b. 9 Feb 1791, Offenbach, Germany
    d. 5 Mar 1861, Georgetown, D.C.
    m. Jane Jacob Belt, 19 Jun 1825, Baltimore, MD
    Service: 1st Masters Mate, Frigate Constellation. 12 May 1812. Acting Master,
        Gunboat No. 74. 12 Aug 1813. Master, Sloop of War, *Erie*. 8 Sep 1814.
    Member - Henry Littleton Page, III [683/4488]

DELAMATER, William
    b. 24/28 Mar 1789, Rhinebeck, NY
    d.
    m. Eliza Douglass, 4 Oct 1817, Rhinebeck, NY
    Service: 1812 - Ensign, 11th Rgt., New York Militia.
            1814 - Lieutenant, 11th Rgt. of New York Militia.
    Member - Nicholas Donnell Ward [619/3591]

DESPEAUX, John
    b. 1796, Baltimore, MD
    d. 24 Jul 1826, Baltimore, MD
    m. Rachel Ardrey (Adderley)
    Service: Private, Captain Stiles' Marine Artillery, Maryland Militia.
    Member - James Etchberger Hancock [223/1065]

A CHRONICLE OF SOLDIERS, SEAMEN, AND MARINES

DIEHL, John
    b. 2 Sep 1796, Adams Co., PA
    d. 14 Jul 1867, Gettysburg, PA
    m. Julianna Snyder, 1819, PA
    Service: Private, 15th Rgt., Captain Samuel Wilson's Volunteer Troop of Calvary, Pennsylvania Militia.
    Member - Edwin Theodore Hollinger [612/3774]

DIGGS, Beverly
    b. 16 Feb 1784, Matthews Co., VA
    d. 16 Oct 1862, Baltimore, MD
    m. Maria Ross
    Service: Commanded, Armed barge under Commodore Barney.
    Member - Ross Miles Diggs [174/934]

DIXON, Jeremiah
    b. 1794-5, VA
    d. Aug-Nov 1860, Cole Co., MI
    Service: Ensign, Captain Bradshaw's Company, 4th Rgt., North Carolina Militia. 28 Nov 1814 - 9 Jan 1815.
    Member - William Ray Ward (collateral) [733/4392]

DONALDSON, James Lowry
    b. circa 1781, Monaghan, Ireland
    d. 12 Sep 1814, Battle of North Point, MD
    m. Jane --
    Service: Lieutenant and Adjutant, 27th Rgt., Maryland Militia.
    Member - Donald Franklin Stewart [561/3260]

DORAN, Philip
    b. abt. 1774-1777, Harford Co., MD
    d. circa 1817-1818, Baltimore, MD
    m. Margaret McCarty
    Service: Ensign, Captain John Turner's Company, 42nd Rgt., Maryland Militia. 28 Aug - 26 Sep 1814. Ensign, Captain John Smithson's Company, 42nd Rgt., Maryland Militia. 12-27 Oct 1814, Camp Hampstead Hill.
    Member - Henry Kenneth Bowers (collateral) [716/4768]

A CHRONICLE OF SOLDIERS, SEAMEN, AND MARINES

DORRANCE, George
- b. 20 Apr 1786, Saybrook, CT
- d. 19 Feb 1841, Albion, NY
- m. Anne Olney Warner, 13 Dec 1807, Providence, RI
- Service: Ensign, 3rd Rgt., 2nd Brigade, Massachusetts Militia.
- **Member** - Charles Samuel Dorrance [318/1511]

DORSEY, John Worthington of Caleb
- b. 3 Jan 1791, Three Brothers, MD
- d. 14 Jul 1841, Linwood, MD
- m. Pleasance Ely
- Service: Captain, 32nd Rgt., Maryland Militia.
- **Member** - Brice Marden Dorsey [677/4355]

DORSEY, Jonathan
- b. 1785, MD
- d. 25 Aug 1859, Carroll Co., MD
- m. Nelly Buckingham, 14 Feb 1812, MD
- Service: Lieutenant, Captain C.S. Owing's Company, 30th Rgt., Maryland Militia. 28 Jul 1813.
- **Member** - John Delashmutt Morris [532/2864]

DOUGLAS, George
- b. 24 Jun 1790, Charles Co., MD
- d. 29 Mar 1869, NY
- m. Mary McElderry
- Service: Private, Baltimore Fencibles, 1st Rgt., Maryland Militia.
- **Member** - Benjamin Dun Douglass [151/742]
  - Robert Dun Douglass [149/740]
  - Robert Graham Dun Douglass [150/741]

DOVE, William Geoghegan
- b. 3 Mar 1785, MD
- d. 10 May 1835, Harford Co., MD
- m. Martha Paul, 18 Jan 1816, MD
- Service: Lieutanant, 10th Company, 42nd Rgt., Maryland Militia.
- **Member** - Charles Polk Dorney [319/1512]

A CHRONICLE OF SOLDIERS, SEAMEN, AND MARINES

DOWNING, Howell
    b. 17 Sep 1790, Windham Co., CT
    d. 5 Aug 1845, IN
    m. Harriett Gorsuch
    Service: Private, 5th Rgt., Maryland Militia.
    Member - George Norbury Mackenzie [35/203]

DRAKE, James
    b. 6 May 1795, Washington Co., VA
    d. 15 Jun 1857, Washington Co., Arkansas
    m. Margaret Fields, 4 Jan 1816, Gallton Co. IL
    Service: Private, Captain Craig's Company, Illinois Militia.
        5 May - 2 Dec 1812.
    Member - Eugene Nelson Moore [705/4654]

DUKEHART, Henri Van Arden
    b. 7 Jul 1794, Baltimore, MD
    d. 10 Dec 1866, Baltimore, MD
    m. Mary Ann Murphy, 20 May 1819, Baltimore, MD
    Service: Private, Captain Aisquith's Company, Baltimore Sharpshooters, 1st Rifle
        Battalion, Maryland Militia. 19 Aug - 18 Oct 1814.
    Member - Morton McIlwain Dukehart [382/1822]
        Thomas Van Arden Dukehart [456/2356]

DULANY, Samuel
    b. 19 June 1790, Baltimore, MD
    d. 26 August 1840, Baltimore, MD
    m. Margaret Mackenheimer
    Service: Private, Mechanical Volunteers, 5th Rgt., Maryland Militia.
    Member - John Highenbothom Dulany [93/397]
        John Mason Dulany [48/248]
        William James Clarke Dulany [95/399]
        William Mason Dulany [49/249]
        Clarence Dulany Foster [222/1064]
        Dulany Foster [434/2305]

A CHRONICLE OF SOLDIERS, SEAMEN, AND MARINES

DURST, *Lightfoot* John
    b. 6 Oct 1766, Berks Co., PA
    d. abt. 1 Jan 1840, Garrett Co., MD
    m. Eva Margaret Glotfelty, 26 Sep 1790, Elk Lick Twp, PA
    Service: Rifleman, Rifle Company, 83rd Rgt., Pennsylvania Militia.
    Member - Ross Compton Durst [526/2981]

DUTTON, John
    b.
    d. 29 Sep 1898, MD
    m. Eliza Waltham
    Service: Private, Captain Ringgold's Company, 6th Rgt., Maryland Militia.
        North Point, 12 Sep 1814.
    Member - Thomas Waltham Dutton [31/190]
        Nathan Parks Lowry [36/204]
        Robert Kelly Lowry [40/210]

DUVAL, Barton
    b. 1776, Prince George's Co., MD
    d. 15 Oct 1831, Prince George's Co., MD
    m. Hannah Issac, 26 Nov 1811, Prince George's Co., MD
    Service: Private, Captain Brook's Company, 34th Rgt., Maryland Militia.
    Member - Richard Mareen Duvall [210/1037]
        Robert Warren Knadler (collateral) [524/2979]

DYKINE, David
    b. 1762, NY
    d. 20 Apr 1852,
    Service: Private, Captain Thomas Jackson's Company, New York Militia.
        8 Sep - 14 Dec 1814.
    Member - Ernest L. Snider [697/4460]

A CHRONICLE OF SOLDIERS, SEAMEN, AND MARINES

EICHELBERGER, William
    b. 30 Jun 1791, PA
    d. 15 Aug 1854, Baltimore, MD
    m. Elizabeth Burneston, 18 Oct 1785, Baltimore, MD
    Service: Private, Captain Nicholson's Company, Baltimore Fencibles, Maryland Militia.
    Member - Oliver Birckhead Wight [483/2655]

ELBERT, Samuel
    b. Kent Co., MD
    d. 8 Dec 1815, Baltimore, MD
    m. Ann Cox, 1 Jul 1797, Kent Island, MD
    Service: Private, 27th Rgt., Maryland Militia. Fought at Battle of North Point.
    Member - Brent Dawson Lehmann [535/3026]
        Leslie Sexton Lehmann [502/2790]
        Wallace Kemp Lehmann [507/2851]
        Samuel Henry Sheib [181/949]

ELLIOTT, Abraham James
    b. 22 Jan 1792, Baltimore Co., MD
    d. 19 Oct 1851, Baltimore Co., MD
    m. Margaret Cunningham, 13 Sep 1809, Baltimore Co., MD
    Service: 1st Corporal, 41st Rgt., Maryland Militia.
        25 Aug - 1 Nov 1814.
    Member - Lawrence Bailey Chambers [695/4498]
        Robert Douglas Chambers [710/4704]

ELLIOTT, John
    b. 17--, Queen Annes Co., MD
    d. May 1823, Queen Annes Co., MD
    m. Margaret --, Queen Annes Co., MD
    Service: Captain, 18th Rgt., Maryland Militia. 23 Apr 1813 - Sep 1814.
    Member - Ernest Lewis Pardee [643/4042]

A CHRONICLE OF SOLDIERS, SEAMEN, AND MARINES

ELMENDORF, Martin
    b. 24 Aug 1769, Kingston, NY
    d. 20 Dec 1844, Kingston, NY
    m. Rachel Roosa, 14 Feb 1792, Kingston, NY
    Service: Captain, Lieutenant Colonel Hardenbergh's Rgt., New York Militia.
        19 Sep - 8 Nov 1813.
    Member - William Ten Eyck Elmendorf, Jr. [509/2854]

ELY, George
    b. 1777, Harford Co., MD
    d. OH
    m. Ann Spencer
    Service: Private, 7th Company, 27th Rgt., Maryland Militia.
    Member - Charles Alfred Ely King [127/596]

EMORY, John King Beck
    b. 1792 Queen Anne's Co., MD
    d.
    m. Sara Hopper
    Service: Captain, 38th Rgt., Maryland Militia.
    Member - Thomas Lansdale Berry [255/1176]

ESTES, Triplett Thorp
    b. 1778, VA
    d. circa 1852, Dinwiddie Co., Va
    m. Elizabeth Gibson, VA
    Service: Captain, 8th Rgt., 4th Brigade, Virginia Militia.
        27 Aug 1814 - 19 Feb 1815.
    Member - John William Johnston Estes [549/3127]

ETCHBERGER, William
    b.
    d. 29 Sep 1830, Baltimore, MD
    m. Charlotte Cunningham
    Service: Private, 6th Rgt., Maryland Militia.
    Member - James Etchberger Hancock [223/1065]

A CHRONICLE OF SOLDIERS, SEAMEN, AND MARINES

ETTER, Philip
    b. 9 Jun 1789, Mt. Joy, PA
    d. 31 Aug 1851, Philadelphia, PA
    m. Susanna Margaretha Haller, 16 Nov 1768, Mt. Joy, PA
    Service: Private, Captains Cotter's and Justice P. Bullard's Companies, 1st Rgt., Pennsylvania Militia. 26 Aug - 26 Sep 1814.
    Member - Thomas Clifton Etter, Jr. [729/3134]

EVANS, James
    b. 26 Nov 1785, Cecil Co., MD
    d. 15 Jan 1848, Cecil Co., MD
    m. Mary Patterson, 14 Feb 1814
    Service: Sergeant, Captain Mackey's Company, 49th Rgt. Maryland Militia.
    Member - Frank Barton Evans, Jr. [522/2968]

FAIR, Peter
    b. 15 Jun 1790, Manchester, MD
    d. 14 Dec 1844, Manchester, MD
    m. Barbara Ziegler, 1812, Alesia, MD
    Service: Private, Captain John Kerlenger's Company, Maryland Militia. 19 Aug - 10 Sept 1813.
    Member - Gordon Malvern Fair Stick, Jr. [540/3067]
        Gordon Malvern Fair Stick, Sr. [537/3063]
        Thomas Howard Fitchett Stick [539/3065]

FARNANDIS (Fernandis), Walter
    b. 1782, Charles Co., MD
    d. 11 Feb 1856, Baltimore, MD
    m. Mary Elizabeth Dorsey, 30 May 1816, Baltimore, MD
    Service: Private, Captain Nicholson's Company, Maryland Militia. 19 Aug - 31 Oct 1814.
    Member - W. Walter Farnandis [701/4595]

FERGUSON, William
    b. 16 Aug 1788, Franklin Co., PA
    d. 28 Jan 1885, Cincinnati, OH
    m. Eliza Crouse
    Service: Private, Calvary Company, Ohio Militia.
    Member - Edward Ferguson Arthurs [140/688]

A CHRONICLE OF SOLDIERS, SEAMEN, AND MARINES

FITCH, Jonathan
    b. 25 Jan 1793, Baltimore Co., MD
    d. 2 Apr 1875, Madison, IN
    m. Margaret Clerke, 10 Jun 1823, Baltimore, MD
    Service: 3rd Lieutenant, Baltimore Union Artillery, Maryland Militia.
        15 Jul - 12 Sep 1814.
    Member - Robert Meldrum Riggs [631/3983]

FITZHUGH, Philip
    b. 1790 Caroline Co., VA
    d. Dec 1836, Caroline Co., VA
    m. Mary Macon Aylette, 13 July 1813, Caroline Co., VA
    Service: Corporal, Captain Armestead Hoomes' Company, Virginia Militia.
    Member - Howard Steptoe Fitzhugh, II [481/2641]

FLOWER, Gustavus
    b. abt 1795, St. Mary's Co., MD
    d. abt. Dec 1830, St. Mary's Co., MD
    m. Jane Bean
    Service: Private, 43rd Rgt., Maryland Militia. 14 Jul - 14 Aug 1814.
    Member - John Sebastian Flower [211/1041]

FOBES, Joshua, 2nd
    b. 15 Jan 1789, Bridgewater, MA
    d. 23 Aug 1878, Bridgewater, MA
    m. Chloe Keith, 13 Aug 1809, Bridgewater, MA
    Service: Private, Captain Keith's Company, Massachusetts Militia.
        17 Sep 1814 - 13 Oct 1814.
    Member - Richard Wingate Bauer [497/2765]

FORD, George W.
    b. 29 Oct 1795, Cecil Co., MD
    d. 8 Oct 1887, Cecil Co., MD
    m. Eliza Ann Dorsey
    Service: Private, Independent Artillerist, 1st Rgt., Maryland Militia.
    Member - Howard Hall Macy Lee [111/430]

A CHRONICLE OF SOLDIERS, SEAMEN, AND MARINES

FOUNTAIN, Andrew
    b. 4 Jun 1796, Caroline Co., MD
    d. 15 Jul 1865, Fleming Co., KY
    Service: Private, served as Drummer, Captain DuPont's Company, Delaware Militia. 31 Aug 1814 - Jan 1815.
    Member - Lucien MacDowell Sadtler [394/1909]

FOUNTAIN (Fontaine), Henry
    b. Somerset Co., MD
    d. Somerset Co., MD
    m. Elizabeth Bennett, 9 Apr 1802, Worcester Co., MD
    Service: 1st Lieutenant, Captain Atkinson's Artillery Company, Maryland Militia. 7 Jan - 27 Apr 1814.
    Member - William Henry Pitcher, Jr. [377/1768]

FOWBLE, William
    b.
    d.
    Service: Private, Company of Baltimore Yeagers, 1st Rifle Battalion, Maryland Militia.
    Member - James Wallace McCurley [53/252]

FRENCH, William
    b. abt. 1760, Calvert Co., MD
    d. abt. 1820, Baltimore, MD
    m. Sarah Ann Cully
    Service: Private, Captain Deems' Company, 51st Rgt., Maryland Militia.
    Member - Chester Lee French [202/1021]

FUHRMAN, Philip
    b. 22 Oct 1787, PA
    d. 25 Feb 1841, York Co., PA
    m. Christina Wilhelm, 13 Oct 1807, Hanover, PA
    Service: Private, Captain J. Kerlinger's Company, Maryland Militia. 25 Aug - 27 Oct 1814.
    Member - Henry Hoke Leber [576/3336]

A CHRONICLE OF SOLDIERS, SEAMEN, AND MARINES

FURLONG, William
    b.
    d.
    m. Sarah Johnson
    Service: Private, Captain Stiles' Marine Artillery, Maryland Militia.
    Member - Winfield Peters [101/404]

GEHRING, John George
    b. Germany
    d. 6 Aug 1843, Baltimore, MD
    m. Mary Magdalene Gamerothe
    Service: Private, Baltimore Yeagers, 5th Rgt., Maryland Militia.
    Member - John George Gehring [102/415]

GEORGE, John
    b. circa 1792, Wake Co., NC
    d. 18 Feb 1832, Wake Co., NC
    m. Polly George, 18 Dec 1817, Wake Co., NC
    Service: Private, Captain John R. Clarke's Company, North Carolina Militia.
        18 Jul - 13 Aug 1813.
    Member - Alfred Laland Green (collateral) [723/4801]

GIFFORD, William
    b. 1779, Sullivan Co., NC
    d. 1837, Marshall Co., TN
    m. Ruth Money, Sullivan Co., NC
    Service: Private, Captain Samuel B. Knight's Company, Tennesseee Militia.
        4 Oct 1813 - 4 Jan 1814.
    Member - Benjamin Dunlap Hill, Jr. [544/3086]

GILBERTHORP, William
    b. 9 September 1797, Baltimore, MD
    d. 23 August 1835, York, PA
    m. Sarah --
    Service: Sergeant, Captain Brown's Company, Maryland Militia.
    Member - Joseph Norris Harris [422/2263]

A CHRONICLE OF SOLDIERS, SEAMEN, AND MARINES

GILL, Stephen
    b. 17 Mar 1781, Baltimore Co., MD
    d. 7 Jan 1846, Baltimore Co., MD
    m. Phoebe Osborn
    Service: Captain, 41st Rgt., Maryland Militia. 25 Aug - 1 Nov 1814.
    Member - Nicholas Rufus Gill [112/439]
        Robert Lee Gill [113/440]
        Roger Taney Gill [114/441]

GILL, William Lowry
    b. 21 Dec 1797, Alexandria, VA
    d. 10 Jan 1880, Baltimore, MD
    m. Ann Upshur Ball
    Service: Midshipman, U.S. Navy until 1815.
    Member - William Harrison Gill [52/274]

GILLES, George
    b. 15 Jan 1780, Rewastico Hundred, DE
    d. 15 Jan 1828, Sussex Co., DE
    m. Philis Lowe Waller, 1808
    Service: Private, 9th Rgt., Delaware Militia. 10 Dec 1814 - 3 Mar 1815.
    Member - Melvin James Bradley [673/4284]

GODDARD, Charles
    b. 1794
    d. 1872
    Service: Private, 1st Company, 27th Rgt., Maryland Militia. Wounded severly at North Point.
    Member - Joseph A. Myers [62/305]

GOLDSBOROUGH, Robert Henry
    b. 1779, Talbot Co., MD
    d. 1836, Talbot Co., MD
    Service: Captain, 9th Calvary District, 8 May 1812; promoted to Major on 13 Feb 1813.
    Member - Richard Hooper Goldsborough (collateral) [582/3548]

A CHRONICLE OF SOLDIERS, SEAMEN, AND MARINES

GORE, George
    b. 1791, Baltimore, MD
    d. 8 Jan 1861, Baltimore Co., MD
    m. Catherine W. --
    Service: Private, 6th Calvary Rgt., Maryland Militia.
    Member - Alfred Duncan Bernard [132/627]
        Richard Constable Bernard [290/1424]

GORSUCH, George Washington
    b. 23 Jul 1795, Carroll Co., MD
    d. 26 Jun 1866, Carroll Co., MD
    m. Mary Gardner, 28 Oct 1819
    Service: Corporal, Captain William Frizell's Company, Maryland Militia.
        19 Aug - 10 Sep 1813.
    Member - Charles Ellsworth Moylan, Jr. [550/3128]

GORSUCH, Thomas
    b. 1788, Baltimore, MD
    d. 18 Sep 1874, Baltimore Co., MD
    m. Sarah Wheeler, 17 Dec 1811, Baltimore Co., MD
    Service: Private, Captain Steever's Company, 27 Rgt., Maryland Miltia.
    Member - Oscar Suter Benson [300/1474]

GOUGH, Harry Dorsey
    b.
    d. Baltimore, MD
    Service: Private, Captain Lee's Company, 7th Calvary Rgt., Maryland Militia.
        27 Aug - 2 Sep 1814.
    Member - Harry Gough Dallam [201/1020]

GOULD, James
    b.
    d.
    Service: Private, 1st Baltimore Volunteer Artillery, 1st Rgt., Maryland Militia.
    Member - James Wallace McCurley [53/252]

A CHRONICLE OF SOLDIERS, SEAMEN, AND MARINES

GOVER, Robert
    b. 22 Aug 1769, Baltimore Co., MD
    d. 1843, Harford Co., MD
    m. Cassandra Lee, 4 Nov 1800, Harford Co., MD
    Service: Corporal of an Extra Battalion raised in Harford Co, MD.
    Member - John Bryarly Munnikhuysen [579/3389]

GRAHAM, William
    b.
    d.
    Service: Private, 6th Company, 6th Rgt., Maryland Militia.
    Member - Felix McCurley [51/251]
        James Wallace McCurley [53/252]

GRADY, Anthony
    b. Cork, Ireland
    d. between 1821-1831, Baltimore, MD
    m. Mary Ann Murphy
    Service: Private, 2nd Company, 57th Rgt., Maryland Militia.
    Member - James Aloysius Maloney [86/392]

GRAVES, Jacob
    b. 1 Feb 1779, Orange Co., VA
    d. 6 Jul 1854, Orange Co., VA
    m. Fannie White, 20 Sep 1800, Orange Co., VA
    Service: Captain, War of 1812.
    Member - William Burton Guy, Jr. [492/2732]
        Amos R. Koontz [487/2669]
        James W. Koontz, II [489/2729]

GREEN, Charles Bosley
    b. 1793, Baltimore Co., MD
    d. 28 Mar 1871, Baltimore, MD
    m. Elisabeth McGaw
    Service: Private, Captain Guiton's Company, 2nd Rgt., Maryland Militia.
    Member - Walter Penrose Summers [206/1026]
        Thomas Wilson Williamson [195/995]

A CHRONICLE OF SOLDIERS, SEAMEN, AND MARINES

GREEN, Grief
    b. 23 Jun 1770, VA
    d. 14 Jul 1846, Mecklenburg, VA
    m. Eliza Aperson, VA
    Service: Lieutenant Colonel, 98th Rgt., Virginia Militia. 31 Jul 1813.
        6th Rgt., Virginia Militia. 14 Aug 1813 - 15 Jan 1814.
    Member - Samuel Hamilton Spragins, Jr. [667/4211]
        Samuel Hamilton Spragins, III [692/4610]

GREEN, Samuel
    b. 30 Jan 1762, Shropshire, England
    d. 7 Nov 1823, Baltimore, MD
    m. Hannah Naylor, 24 Jul 1796, Baltimore, MD
    Service: Private, Captain Christian Adreon's Company, Union Volunteers, Maryland Militia. September 1814.
    Member - Joseph Elliott Green, Jr. [430/2300]

GREER, George
    b. Belfast, Ireland
    d. 1826, Baltimore, MD
    m. Mary Hall
    Service: Private, Baltimore Independent Artillerists, Maryland Militia.
    Member - Charles Christian Baughman [184/961]
        Emilius Allen Baughman [185/962]
        Greer Harry Baughman [183/960]

GRIFFITH, Howard
    b. 7 Jun 1794, Montgomery Co., MD
    d. 10 Oct 1866, Baltimore, MD
    m. Jemina Jacob, 8 Feb 1782, Montgomery Co., MD
    Service: Private, Baltimore Independent Blues, Maryland Militia.
    Member - Louis P. Griffith [2/9]

GRIFFITH, Lyde
    b. 13 Jan 1774, Montgomery Co., MD
    d. 28 Jun 1839, Montgomery Co., MD
    m. Anne Poole, 9 Jan 1808
    Service: Captain, 44th Rgt., Maryland Militia. 20 Aug 1814.
    Member - Milton Wickers Davis, Jr. [514/2858]

A CHRONICLE OF SOLDIERS, SEAMEN, AND MARINES

GRIFFITH, Thomas
    b. after 1776, Anne Arundel Co., MD
    d. before 26 May 1838, Anne Arundel Co., MD
    m. Harriet Worthington Simpson, 17 Jan 1811, Anne Arundel Co., MD
    Service: Captain, 32nd Rgt., Maryland Militia. 21 Oct 1812.
    Member - Griffith Fontaine Pitcher [500/2767]
        Charles Francis Stein, Jr. [420/2239]

GRIM, Jonathan
    b. 1784 (?), MD
    d. between 1822-1840, OH
    m. Elizabeth Long
    Service: Private, Captain Joseph Chews' Company, 2nd Rgt., Ohio Militia.
        8 May - 18 Aug 1813.
    Member - Robert Elroy Grim [725/4586]

GRINDALL, John Gibson
    b. Harford Co., MD
    d. IL
    m. Ellen Wheeler
    Service: Private, Captain Smithson's Detachment, 40th Rgt., Maryland Militia.
        26 Apr - 4 May 1813. Private, Captain Amoss' Company, 42nd Rgt., Maryland
        Militia. 29 Aug - 26 Sep 1814.
    Member - Charles Sylvester Grindall [208/1028]

GROVE, Reuben
    b. 25 Mar 1795, PA
    d. 7 Feb 1878, Frederick, MD
    m. Maria Lantz
    Service: Private, Captain John Brengle's Company, Camp Diehl, Baltimore, MD.
        2 Sep - 6 Nov 1814.
    Member - Charles Edward Kemp [708/4707]

GURNEY, Gridley
    b. 24 Apr 1794, Abington, MA
    d. after 1851
    m. Mary Griffin, 18 Jun 1823, Dorchester Co., MD
    Service: Private, 2nd Rgt., MA Militia.
    Member - John Thomas Gurney, 3rd [633/3984]

A CHRONICLE OF SOLDIERS, SEAMEN, AND MARINES

GWIN, James
    b. 1769, NC
    d. 3 Aug 1841, Vicksburg, MS
    Service: Chaplain, Brigadier General Coffee's Brigade of Volunteer Gunmen, Tennessee Militia. 28 Sep 1814 - 27 Apr 1815.
    Member - Alvin K. Baskette [379/1807]

HALBERT, William
    b. 23 Nov 1793, Goshen, MA
    d. between 1855-67, Leroy, NY
    Service: Private, Captain Chauncey Bild's Company, New York Militia on the Niagara Frontier.
    Member - James William Halbert (collateral) [675/4285]
        Virgil Allen Halbert (collateral) [605/3697]

HALL, Joseph
    b. Falmouth, England
    d. Baltimore, MD
    m. Elizabeth Levly
    Service: Private, Sea Fencibles, Maryland Militia.
    Member - Joseph Cotton Hall [32/191]

HALL, Thomas William
    b. 7 Jul 1793, Culpeper Co., VA
    d. 15 Oct 1872, Baltimore, MD
    m. Elizabeth Stickney Ward, 22 May 1832, Baltimore, MD
    Service: Captain, Company of Rifleman, 5th Rgt., Virginia Militia. Jan - May 1814.
    Member - Clayton Colman Hall [262/1199]

HAMMOND, Lloyd Thomas
    b. 11 Aug 1779, Anne Arundel Co., MD
    d. 12 May 1838, Anne Arundel Co., MD
    m. Barbara Arianna Raitt, Anne Arundel Co., MD
    Service: Paymaster, 32nd Rgt., Maryland Militia.
    Member - Edward Hammond [308/1496]

A CHRONICLE OF SOLDIERS, SEAMEN, AND MARINES

HAMPTON, Thomas
    b. 25 Dec 1786, VA
    d. 31 Jul 1843, Franklin Co., KY
    m. Emily Pemberton Jones, 30 Sep 1824, Frankfort, KY
    Service: Private, Baker's Company, 1st Rgt., U.S. Infantry.
    Member - George Long Smith [251/1165]

HARRIS, Benjamin James
    b. Richmond, VA
    d. 1834, Florence, Al
    m. Sarah Ellyson
    Service: Private, Captain McCabes' Company, 19th Rgt., Virginia Militia.
    Member - Charles Henry Hardin Branch [147/724]
        Henry Branch [146/723]

HARRIS, David
    b. 23 Jul 1770, Baltimore, MD
    d. 4 Feb 1844, Jefferson Co., VA
    m. Sarah Montgomery, 11 Nov 1798
    Service: Lieutenant Colonel, 1st Rgt., Maryland Militia.
    Member - William Hall Harris [242/1148]
        William Hall Harris, Jr. [283/1385]

HARRISON, Stephen
    b. 1791, Talbot Co., MD
    d. 1845, Talbot Co., MD
    m. Susanna Spencer, 15 Dec 1818, Talbot Co., MD
    Service: Private, Captain Smith's Company, 51st Rgt., Maryland Militia.
    Member - Henry Christopher Harrison, Jr. [486/2658]
        Howard MacCarthy, Jr. [488/2670]

HARRISON, Thomas Edward
    b. 1786, St. Mary's Co., MD
    d. 1866, St. Mary's Co., MD
    Service: Sergeant, Captain Sothoron's Detachment, 45th Rgt., Maryland Militia.
        21 Apr - 1 May 1813.
    Member - George Harrison [372/1729]

A CHRONICLE OF SOLDIERS, SEAMEN, AND MARINES

HAUCK (Houck), William
    b. 1781, Carroll Co., MD
    d. 27 Mar 1854, Houcksville, MD
    m. Catherine Frank
    Service: Captain, Sixth Cavalry District, Maryland Militia. 22 April 1814.
    Member - Charles Herman Williams [581/3442]
        Mark Mansfield Williams [668/4212]

HAY, Peter
    b. 21 Nov 1789, Philadelphia, PA
    d. 15 Nov 1879, Philadelphia, PA
    m. Elizabeth C. --
    Service: Private, Philadelphia Junior Artillerists, Pennsylvania Militia.
        23 Mar - 7 Apr 1813.
    Member - Randall Groves Hay [446/1948]

HAYES, Walter Cody
    b. 1778, Ireland
    d. 10 Mar 1826, Charleston, SC
    m. Maria Barbara Wonderly
    Service: Private, Marine Artillery, Maryland Militia.
    Member - Edwin Abbott Colbert [235/1130]
        Philip Maulsby Colbert [343/1602]
        James Carroll LeGrand Cole [115/442]

HENDERSON, Peter H.
    b. abt. 1790, Eastern Shore, VA
    d. 14 Mar 1835, Baltimore, MD
    m. Mary Booth, 29 Oct 1815, Baltimore, MD
    Service: Private, Captain Haubert's Company, 51st Rgt., Maryland Militia.
    Member - Charles Franklin Henderson [212/1042]
        Charles Griffin Henderson [296/1455]
        George Washington Henderson [315/1504]

A CHRONICLE OF SOLDIERS, SEAMEN, AND MARINES

HILDT, John
    b. 1775, Hanover, Germany
    d. 1862, OH
    m. Elizabeth Weller
    Service: Ensign, Captain Stewart's Company, 51st Rgt., Maryland Militia.
    Member - John C. Hildt [218/1055]
        Thomas Hildt [219/1056]

HILL, Thomas Gardner
    b. Aug 1793, Philadelphia, PA
    d. 31 Dec 1849, Baltimore, MD
    m. Martha Ann Bryant
    Service: 1st Sergeant, 27th Rgt., Maryland Militia.
    Member - Nicholas Sluby Hill [90/394]
        Norman Alan Hill [399/2070]
        Samuel Emory Hill [81/379]
        Thomas Hill [80/378]
        James Armstrong Owings Tucker [96/400]

HITE, James Madison
    b.
    d. 1859, Winchester, VA
    m. Caroline Rose
    Service: Private, Captain Tucker's Troop of Cavalry, 57th Rgt., Virginia Militia.
        26 Aug - 18 Sep 1814.
    Member - Drayton Meade Hite [203/1022]

HOLLYDAY, Henry
    b. 11 Dec 1771, Ratcliffe Manor, MD
    d. 1880, Easton, MD
    m. Ann Carmichael, 1798, Chestertown, MD
    Service: Paymaster, 9th Calvary District, Queen Anne and Talbot Co., Maryland
        Militia. 1 Dec 1813.
    Member - Thomas James Hollyday [670/4214]

A CHRONICLE OF SOLDIERS, SEAMEN, AND MARINES

HOOPER, James [60/290]
    b. 5 Jul 1804, Baltimore, MD
    d. 14 Mar 1898, Baltimore, MD
    m. Ann Elizabeth Brannan, 27 Dec 1824, Baltimore, MD
    Service: "Powder Monkey" (Coxswain) on Schooner, *Comet*.
        4 Jul 1812 - 4 Sep 1814.
    Member - Thomas Lee Dorsey, Sr. [609/3776]
        Vachel Paul Dorsey [629/3971]

HOPPER, Daniel Cox
    b. 29 Mar 1777, Queen Anne's Co., MD
    d. 1849, Queen Anne's Co., MD
    m. Maria Thomas, 15 Jan 1805, Queen Anne's Co., MD
    Service: First Lieutenant, 38th Rgt., Maryland Militia.
    Member - William Nussear Stevenson Pugh [530/2997]
        William Nussear Stevenson Pugh, Jr. [584/3446]

HOSHALL, Jesse, II
    b. 4 Apr 1786, Baltimore Co., MD
    d. 9 Sep 1876, Baltimore Co., MD
    Service: First Lieutenant, Captain Isaac Raven's Company, 2nd Rgt.,
        Maryland Militia. 14 Oct - 1 Dec 1814.
    Member - Frank Bertram Scott (collateral) [546/3089]

HOUCK, John
    b. 19 Jan 1785, Baltimore Co., MD
    d. 17 Jul 1873, Baltimore Co., MD
    m. Mary Wolf
    Service: Private, Captain Stockdale's Company, 36th Rgt., Maryland Militia.
        21 Aug - 27 Oct 1814.
    Member - George Wesley Houck [331/1553]
        Harry Elijah Houck [332/1554]

HOWISON, Alexander
    b. 18 Nov 1773, Prince William Co., VA
    d. 1825, (?) VA
    m. Ann Garland, 1799, VA
    Service: Captain, 36th Rgt., Virginia Militia.
    Member - Gregory Howison Green [709/4708]
        Samuel Alexander Green, Jr. [516/2907]

A CHRONICLE OF SOLDIERS, SEAMEN, AND MARINES

HUGHES, Thomas
    b. 21 Jan 1789, Greene Co., PA
    d. 20 Jun 1849, Wheeling, VA
    m. Mary Odenbaugh, 15 Mar 1815, Wheeling, VA
    Service: Private, Captain John Brown's Company, Pennsylvania Militia.
        24 Sep 1812 - 22 Apr 1813.
    Member - Adrian Hughes [320/1513]

HULSE, John
    b. 1791, Lancaster, England
    d. 8 Oct 1864, Baltimore, MD
    m. Elizabeth Ann Barton
    Service: 3rd Corporal, Sharp Shooters, 1st Rifle Battalion, Maryland Militia.
    Member - William Brinkett Hulse [108/427]

HUME, Charles
    b. Orange Co., VA
    d. Trimble Co., KY
    m. Celia Shumate, 1 Jun 1803, Farquier Co., VA
    Service: Lieutenant, Captain Joseph Hume's Company, 1st Rgt., Virginia Militia.
        4 Aug - 17 Dec 1814.
    Member - Edgar Erskine Hume, Jr. [247/1128]

HUNT, Eustace
    b. 26 Nov 1789, Halifax Co., VA
    d. 18 Sep 1845, Pitts Co., VA
    m. Eliza Anderson Glenn
    Service: Ensign (2nd Lieutenant) Captain Howerton's Company, 5th Rgt., Virginia
        Militia. 1 Jun - 1 Dec 1814.
    Member - Robert Smith Phifer, Jr. [178/945]

HUSH, Samuel
    b.
    d. 25 Dec 1814, Baltimore, MD
    m. Mary Fletcher
    Service: Private, Captain Magee's Company, 1st Rgt., Maryland Militia.
        Died from wounds received at the Battle of Bladensburg.
    Member - Samuel Fletcher Primrose [17/178]

A CHRONICLE OF SOLDIERS, SEAMEN, AND MARINES

HUSTER, Gotlieb
    b. 19 Nov 1775
    d. 28 Aug 1868, Baltimore Co., MD
    m. Elizabeth Davis, 26 Nov 1826, Baltimore, MD
    Service: Private, Captain Hanna's Fells Point Light Dragoons, 5th Calvary, Maryland Militia.
    Member - Ernest Elmer Wooden [425/2277]

HYLAND, Henry M.
    b. 1796, Kent Co., MD
    d. Sep 1851
    m. Marcia Grant
    Service: Private, Kent Co. Company, Maryland Militia.
    Member - James Hyland [11/14]

IGLEHART, Jesse
    b. 18 Feb 1781, Montgomery Co., MD
    d. 21 Apr 1854, Montgomery Co., MD
    m. Sarah Burton, 5 Dec 1810, Montgomery Co., MD
    Service: Private, 22nd Rgt., Maryland Militia. 28 July 1813 - 1 September 1813.
    Member - Harold Edgar Wilmoth [740/4914]

IJAMS, John
    b. 3 Apr 1789, Frederick Co., MD
    d. 31 Aug 1879, Baltimore Co., MD
    m. Catherine Barnes, 27 Apr 1812, Baltimore Co., MD
    Service: Private, Captain James Foster's Company, 51st Rgt., Maryland Militia. 23 - 30 August 1813. 1st Lieutenant, Captain Foster's Company, 19 Aug - 18 Nov 1814.
    Member - George Edwin Ijams [391/1887]
        George Edwin Ijams, Jr. [427/2291]

INLOES, William
    b. 14 Nov 1787
    d. 1854
    m. Mary Sewell
    Service: 1st Lieutenant, 6th Rgt., Maryland Militia.
    Member - Henry Snow [349/1635]

A CHRONICLE OF SOLDIERS, SEAMEN, AND MARINES

JACKSON, David Edward
    b. 30 Oct 1788, Lewis Co., VA
    d. 24 Dec 1838, Paris, TN
    m. Juliet Norris, 31 Oct 1809, Harrison Co., VA
    Service: Ensign, Captain Alexander's Company, 1st Rgt., Ohio Militia.
        21 Sep 1812 - 8 Dec 1812.
    Member - Elmer Martin Jackson, Jr. [719/4786]

JENKINS, Edward
    b. 27 Mar 1774, Long Green, MD
    d. 14 Apr 1833, Baltimore, MD
    m. Ann Spalding, 15 Feb 1803
    Service: Private, Independent Company, 5th Rgt., Maryland Militia.
    Member - Edward Austin Jenkins [131/614]
        Francis de Sales Jenkins [130/613]
        Alfred Jenkins Shriver [260/1187]

JENKINS, Felix
    b. 18 Oct 1786, Charles Co., MD
    d. 27 Aug 1838, Baltimore, MD
    m. Frances Helen Wheeler, 23 Sep 1822, Baltimore, MD
    Service: Private, Captain Moale's Company, Columbian Artillery, Maryland Militia.
    Member - Benjamin Wheeler Jenkins [261/1198]
        Edward Felix Jenkins [519/2965]
        Thomas Worthington Offutt [361/1700]

JENKINS, John J.
    b. 17 Oct 1784, Charles Co., MD
    d. 2 Jan 1845, Charles Co., MD
    m. Mary Ann Plowdon, 20 Feb 1808, St. Mary's Co., MD
    Service: Sergeant, Captain John Barnes's Artillery Company, 5th Brigade, Maryland Militia.
    Member - Edward Austin Jenkins [131/614]
        Eugene Augustine Jenkins, Jr. [653/4113]
        Francis de Sales Jenkins [130/613]

A CHRONICLE OF SOLDIERS, SEAMEN, AND MARINES

JENKINS, William
    b. 1767, Baltimore, MD
    d. 19 Feb 1843, Baltimore, MD
    m. Eleanor Wilcox, 1801, Chester Co., PA
    Service: Sergeant, Captain Thompson's Company of Cavalry, Maryland MIlitia. 19 Aug - 30 Nov 1814.
    Member - Michael Jenkins [250/1164]

JENNINGS, James
    b. Lynchburg, VA
    d. Lynchburg, Va
    m. Mary Hawkins, 29 Dec 1831, Lynchburg, VA
    Service: Private, Company B, Virginia Militia. 29 Dec 1813 - 11 Apr 1814.
    Member - Charles Burch Athey [471/2577]

JETT, Thomas H.
    b. circa 1788, Northumberland Co., VA
    d. before 1849, Northumberland Co., VA
    m. Mary Elizabeth Edwards, 9 Apr 1808, Northumberland Co., VA
    Service: Ensign, Virginia Militia.
    Member - Robert Samuel Jett, Jr. [567/3274]

JOHNSON, Samuel
    b. 24 Feb 1797, Knoxville, TN
    d. 21 Jan 1871, Baltimore, MD
    m. Josephine Gonzales
    Service: Private, Captain Piper's United Maryland Artillery. Musician, Captain Spicer's Company, Maryland Militia. 14 Sept 1814.
    Member - E. Richard Coleman [504/2792]

JONES, Hugh
    b. 23 Dec 1791, Harford Co., MD
    d. 1 Mar 1864, Harford Co., MD
    m. Rebecca Ann Kidd, 27 Dec 1821, Cecil Co., MD
    Service: Private, 40th Rgt. Maryland Militia. Apr 1813.
    Member - Carroll Creswell Hopkins [442/2323]
        Joseph Carroll Hopkins [458/2487]

A CHRONICLE OF SOLDIERS, SEAMEN, AND MARINES

JONES, John
    b. 4 Sep 1755, Dorchester Co., MD
    d. 7 Feb 1848, Dorchester Co., MD
    Service: Lieutenant Colonel, 48th Rgt., Maryland Militia.
    Member - Maurice Edward Skinner [384/1828]

JONES, Uriah
    b. 27 May 1788, Baltimore, MD
    d. 21 Oct 1859, Baltimore, MD
    m. Ann Mincher
    Service: Private, Captain Deem's Company, Maryland Militia.
    Member - Henry Jones Ford [196/996]

JONES, William Robinson
    b. 9 Apr 1786, Baltimore, MD
    d. 23 Apr 1857, Baltimore, MD
    m. Jemima Corum
    Service: Purser Stewart, U.S. Navy.
    Member - Hugh Burgess Jones [98/402]

JORDAN, William
    b. 20 Jun 1794, Baltimore, MD
    d. 30 Jun 1853, Carroll Co., MD
    Service: Private, Captain Gorsuch's Company, Maryland Militia.
        26 Jun - 13 Oct 1814.
    Member - Henry Theodore Collenberg, Jr. [408/2164]

KAUFFMAN, Jonathan
    b. abt. 1796, Baltimore, MD
    d. 17 Mar 1850, Frederick Co., MD
    m. Elizabeth Metzger
    Service: Private, Captain Haubert's Company, 51st Rgt., Maryland Militia.
        19 Aug - 18 Nov 1814.
    Member - John Williams Kauffman [180/947]

A CHRONICLE OF SOLDIERS, SEAMEN, AND MARINES

KELL, Thomas
    b. 22 Sep 1772, Baltimore Co., MD
    d. 8 Mar 1846, Baltimore, MD
    m. Mary Ann Goldsmith
    Service: 1st Lieutenant, Independent Light Dragoons, Maryland Militia.
    Member - Samuel Webster Bradford [205/1025]

KELLY, James
    b. Ireland
    d. Philadelphia, PA
    Service: Private, Northern Liberties Washington Rifle Rangers, 2nd Brigade, Pennsylvania Militia.
    Member - Irving Washington Kelly [270/1251

KELSO, John R.
    b. 31 Mar 1791, Baltimore, MD
    d. Nov 1880, Baltimore, MD
    m. Martha Balderston, 1821, Baltimore, MD
    Service: 4th Corporal, Washington Blues, 5th Rgt., Maryland Militia.
    Member - Edmund Joseph Webb, Jr. [314/1500]

KEMP, Frederick
    b. 7 Aug 1780, Frederick, MD
    d. 28 May 1848, Frederick, MD
    m. Margaret Brunner, 15 Apr 1805, Frederick, MD
    Service: Private, Captain Getzendanner's Company, 16th Rgt., 9th Brigade, Maryland Militia. Mar - Oct 1813.
    Member - Charles Edward Kemp [708/4707]

KEMP, Joseph
    b. 14 Jun 1781, Talbot Co., MD
    d. 24 Aug 1835, Baltimore, MD
    m. Anne Cooper
    Service: Captain, 26th Rgt., Maryland Militia.
    Member - Alan Kemp Dolliver [558/3185]
                Wallace Kemp Lehmann [507/1285]

A CHRONICLE OF SOLDIERS, SEAMEN, AND MARINES

KEMP, Thomas
    b. 28 Feb 1779, Talbot Co., MD
    d. 3 Mar 1824, Talbot Co., MD
    m. Rachel Denny
    Service: Private, Captain Kierstead's Company, 6th Rgt., Maryland Militia.
    Member - Edgar Harrison Bennett [494/2733]

KENLY, Edward
    b. 22 Nov 1788, Harford Co., MD
    d. 29 Apr 1861, Baltimore, MD
    m. Maria Keener Reese
    Service: Private, Company C, 27th Rgt., Maryland Militia.
    Member - William Watkins Kenly [170/924]

KENT, Robert Wheeler
    b. 1777, Calvert Co., MD
    d. 2 Nov 1843, South River, MD
    m. Mary Ann MacKubin (Maccubbin), 7 Jun 1814, Annapolis, MD
    Service: Captain, 14 Rgt., U.S. Infantry under Colonel William H. Winder.
        12 Mar 1812.
    Member - Thomas Carroll Worthington, Jr. [679/4357]

KEPLINGER, Michael
    b. 1766, PA
    d. 20 Feb 1849, Baltimore, MD
    Service: Private, Captain Chalmers Company, 51st Rgt., Maryland Militia.
    Member - John Bernard Keplinger [117/489]

KERSHNER, Conrad
    b. 3 Nov 1786, Berks Co., PA
    d. 13 Jul 1848, Schuylkill Co., PA
    m. Barbara Fenstermacher, 1 Jan 1811, Lehigh Co., PA
    Service: Private, Captain Abraham Rinker's Company, 1st Rifle Rgt., Pennsylvania
        Militia. 13 - 26 Nov 1814.
    Member - Raymond Nathan Zimmerman, Jr. [741/4915]

A CHRONICLE OF SOLDIERS, SEAMEN, AND MARINES

KEY, Francis Scott
    b. 1 Aug 1779, Frederick Co., MD
    d. 11 Jan 1843, Baltimore, MD
    m. Mary Tayloe Lloyd, 1802, Annapolis, MD
    Service: Lieutenant and Quartermaster, Major Peter's Georgetown Field Artillery, District of Columbia Militia. 9 Jun - 1 Jul 1814.
    Member - Francis Scott Key Smith [330/1540]

KIMBERLY, Natahaniel
    b. 23 Jan 1775, New Haven, CT
    d. 19 Feb 1836, Baltimore, MD
    m. Mabel --
    Service: Private, Washington Blues, Maryland Militia.
    Member - Albert Kimberly Hadel [5/11]

KING, Samuel
    b. 26 Oct 1758, Somerset Co., MD
    d. 5 Feb 1838, Somerset Co., MD
    m. Elizabeth Waggaman, 2 Sep 1779, Somerset Co., MD
    Service: Sergeant, Captain Heath's Company, 23rd Rgt., Maryland Militia.
    Member - Wilson King Barnes [557/3164]

KLEIN, Lewis
    b. 15 Mar 1783, Frederick, MD
    d. 14 Apr 1837, Loudon Co., VA
    m. Elizabeth Conrad
    Service: Private, Virginia Militia. 23 Aug - 16 Sep 1813.
    Member - Arthur Miller Easter [38/208]
        James Miller Easter [224/1070]

KLINEFELTER, Michael
    b. 20 Feb 1770, York Co., PA
    d. 20 Sep 1850, York Co., PA
    m. Mary Magdalena Gartman, 27 Mar 1796, York, PA
    Service: Private, Captain Pennington's Company, Baltimore Independent Artillerists, Maryland Militia.
    Member - Arthur Klinefelter [527/2982]

A CHRONICLE OF SOLDIERS, SEAMEN, AND MARINES

KLUNK, Peter
    b. Hanover, PA
    d.
    m. M. Louisa Ketterman, York, PA
    Service: Private, Captain Haubert's Company, 51st Rgt., Maryland Militia.
    Member - Louis W. Klunk [280/1368]

KNORR, William
    b. 25 Jun 1788, PA
    d. 16 Jul 1861, Baltimore, MD
    m. Elizabeth Mines, circa 1809
    Service: Private, Captain Peter Pinney's Company, 27th Rgt., Maryland Militia.
        19 Aug - 18 Nov 1814.
    Member - Norman John Knorr [739/4910]
        Sheldon Henry Knorr [735/4888]

KNOTT, Edward
    b. 17 Oct 1790, Montgomery Co., MD
    d. 6 Aug 1866, Baltimore, MD
    m. Elizabeth Sprigg Sweney
    Service: Ensign & Lieutenant, Maryland Militia.
    Member - Aloysius Leo Knott [134/649]

KNOWLES, William
    b. 19 Apr 1785, Sussex Co., DE
    d. 3 Dec 1857, Sussex Co., DE
    m. Nelly Collins
    Service: Private, Captain Rider's Company, Delaware Militia.
    Member - Madison Marine [169/921]
        Richard Elliott Marine [168/920]
        William Matthew Marine [123/558]

A CHRONICLE OF SOLDIERS, SEAMEN, AND MARINES

KOLB, John William
    b. 17 Feb 1776, Frederick Co., MD
    d. 25 Jan 1835, Frederick Co., MD
    m. Maria Eve Ann Miller, 7 Dec 1797, Frederick, MD
    Service: Lieutenant, Captain Bringle's and Captain Mackey's Company, 16 Rgt., Maryland Militia.
    Member - John Devine Cobb, Jr. [451/2345]
          Samuel Robert Fowler, Jr. [459/2551]
          Charles Edward Mealy Kolb [638/4004]
          David William Kolb [452/2346]
          David William Kolb, VI [654/4114]
          Stanely Denmead Kolb [411/2208]
          Stanley Denmead Kolb, Jr. [449/2343]

LAKE, George
    b. 1776, Dorchester Co., MD
    d. 21 Nov 1831, Dorchester Co., MD
    m. Mary Boyne Slacum
    Service: Captain, 48th Rgt., Maryland Militia.
    Member - Richard Pinkney Lake [157/792]

LAKE, Washington
    b. 1784, Dorchester Co., MD
    d. 4 Jun 1826, Dorchester Co., MD
    m. Margaret Slacum
    Service: Lieutenant, Captain George Lakes' Detachment, 48th Rgt., Maryland Militia. 10 Apr 1813 - 20 Jan 1815.
    Member - Richard Pinkney Lake [157/792]

LAMB, John
    b. NC
    d. 4 Dec 1844, Sampson Co., NC
    m. Rebecca Bass, 2 Dec 1814, Sampson Co., NC
    Service: Private, North Carolina Militia. Jul 1813.
    Member - Edwin Williams Southerland [598/3580]

A CHRONICLE OF SOLDIERS, SEAMEN, AND MARINES

LAND, Nathaniel Drew
    b. Sussex Co., VA
    d. 3 Jan 1840, Sussex Co., VA
    m. Mary Hart Rochelle, 26 Aug 1816, VA
    Service: Sergeant, 1st Rgt., Virginia Militia.
    Member - Calvin Shelton Baker [586/3471]

LANDSTREET, John
    b. Amsterdam, Holland
    d. abt. 1855, Baltimore, MD
    m. Anne V. Orme
    Service: Private, Washington Artillery, Maryland Militia.
    Member - John Landstreet [182/950]

LANGHORNE, Maurice
    b. 1787, Cumberland Co., VA
    d. 27 Feb 1865, VA
    m. Elizabeth Allen
    Service: 2nd Lieutenant, Captain Milber's Troop of Cavalry, McDowell's Flying Camp, Virginia Militia. 29 Jun - 2 Oct 1813.
    Member - Charles McIndoe Langhorne [186/963]

LAUGHTER, John L.
    b. 17 Mar 1786, Warren Co., NC
    d. 8 Jan 1858, Warren Co., NC
    m. Ann Hunt
    Service: Captain, 1st Rgt., North Carolina Militia.
    Member - William Hunt Laughter [61/293]

LAWRENCE, Thomas Leggett
    b. 10 Mar 1789, Baltimore, MD
    d.
    m. -- Durham
    Service: Captain, 6th Rgt., Maryland Militia. 12 Jul 1814.
    Member - Lawrence Irvin Ashley [445/2340]

A CHRONICLE OF SOLDIERS, SEAMEN, AND MARINES

LEAKIN, Shepherd Church
  b. 23 Apr 1790, Baltimore Co., MD
  d. Nov 1867, Baltimore Co., MD
  m. Margaret Dobbin
  Service: Captain, 38th U.S. Infantry. 20 May 1813 - 15 Jun 1815.
  Member - St. George Charles Leakin Sioussat [265/1223]

LEARY, Peter
  b. 26 Feb 1781, Baltimore, MD
  d. 4 Feb 1871, Baltimore, MD
  m. Eliza Hagerman, 1812, Baltimore, MD
  Service: Lieutenant, Captain Warner's Company, 39th Rgt., Maryland Militia.
  Member - Peter Leary [137/685]
    Rudolph William Leary [328/1538]
    William Emory Waring, Jr. [172/932]

LEAYCROFT, Viner
  b. 17--, New York, NY
  d. 1813, Sackett's Harbor, NY
  Service: Killed at the Battle of Sackett's Harbor.
  Member - George Grenville Merrill (collateral) [587/3455]

LeCOMPTE, Joseph
  b. circa 1775, Dorchester Co., MD
  d. 14 Jan 1836, Dorchester Co., MD
  m. -- Brannock
  Service: Private, Captain Roger Woolford's Company, 10th Calvary District, Maryland Militia. 14 - 17 Apr 1813.
  Member - Harry Lloyd LeCompte, Jr. [724/4812]

LEIPER, George Gray
  b. 3 Feb 1786, Leiperville, PA
  d. 27 Nov 1868, Delaware Co., PA
  M. Eliza Snowden Thomas, 3 May 1810, Fairland, MD
  Service: Lieutenant, Delaware County Fensibles, Pennsylvania Militia. Commissioned 21 Sep 1814.
  Member - Caleb Winslow, Jr. [736/4889]
    Caleb Winslow, Sr. [580/3398]
    John Leiper Winslow, Jr. [666/4210]
    Nathan John Winslow [689/4493]

A CHRONICLE OF SOLDIERS, SEAMEN, AND MARINES

LEWMAN, Noah
    b. 1773, MD
    d. after 1829
    m. Mary Ann Harrison
    Service: Private, Captain Stocton's Company, U.S. 28th Infantry.
        15 May 1813 - 6 Jul 1814.
    Member - Willard Gerald Saunders, II [684/4489]

LINTHICUM, Abner
    b. 7 Jul 1763, Anne Arundel Co., MD
    d. 19 Feb 1848, Anne Arundel Co., MD
    m. Rachel Jacob(s), 3 Jan 1791, Baltimore Co., MD
    Service: Major, Anne Arundel Co. Company, Maryland Militia. 23 Mar 1814.
    Member - Carville D. Benson [597/3624]
        John Oregon Benson [493/2763]
        George Milton Linthicum [380/1808]
        John Charles Linthicum [374/1765]
        Sweetser Linthicum [639/4040]

LINTHICUM, Charles Griffith
    b. 10 Mar 1788, Anne Arundel Co., MD
    d.
    m. Louisa Meriweather, 15 Apr 1810, Frederick Co., MD
    Service: Adjutant, 32nd Rgt., Maryland Militia.
    Member - George Emory Linthicum, III [545/3088]

LINVILLE, James M.
    b. 1781
    d. 1837
    m. Mariah Long
    Service: Private, Captain Moale's Company, Columbia Artillery, Maryland Militia.
    Member - Charles Hardesty Linville [259/1180]

A CHRONICLE OF SOLDIERS, SEAMEN, AND MARINES

LLOYD, Edward IV
    b. 22 Jul 1779, Talbot Co., MD
    d. 2 Jun 1834, Annapolis, MD
    m. Sally Scott Murray, 30 Nov 1797
    Service: [State Senator, 1812-1814]
    Member - Franklin Buchanan Owen [305/1492]

LLOYD, James III
    b. abt. 1742, Talbot Co., MD
    d. abt. 1815, Talbot Co., MD
    m. Sarah Martin, prior 1769, Talbot Co., MD
    Service: General in command of the Eastern Shore Division, Maryland Militia.
    Member - Leslie William Chittenden [450/2344]

LOCKETT, Samuel Locke
    b. 3 Jul 1782, VA
    d. 10 Dec 1850, Mecklenburg, VA
    m. Selina Ann Watkins, 8 Jan 1811, Prince Edward Co., VA
    Service: Cornet, Captain Samuel L. Allen's Troop of Cavalry, 1st Rgt.,
        Virginia Militia. 29 Jun 1813 - 18 Sep 1814.
    Member - Robert Wynter Davies [691/4500]

LONG, Jesse
    b. 1793, Worcester Co., MD
    d. 3 April 1857, Williamsport, MD
    m. Elizabeth Geyert
    Service: Private, Washington Blues, Maryland Militia.
    Member - Samuel Burkett Long [26/184]
        William F. Long [19/180]

LUMBERSON, John [120/513]
    b. 11 May 1806, near Knoxville, TN
    d. 5 Feb 1898
    Service: Drummer, Company N, 1st Battalion, U.S. Corps of Artillery.
        1 Sep 1813 - 13 Aug 1837.

A CHRONICLE OF SOLDIERS, SEAMEN, AND MARINES

LYNCH, Patrick of William
    b. 1794, Baltimore Co., MD
    d. 15 Feb 1869, Baltimore Co., MD
    m. Mary Ann Howlett, 8 Jun 1820, Baltimore Co., MD
    Service: Private, Captain Archibald Dobbins Company, Maryland Militia.
        19 Aug - 18 Nov 1814.
    Member - James Miller Merritt [569/3278]

MacARTHUR, Charles Gilderoy
    b. 1781
    d. 1869
    Service: Sergeant in Captain Pettis' Company, 4th Rgt., Vermont Militia.
        1 Sep - 8 Dec 1812.
    Member - Douglas MacArthur [506/2808]

MacDONOUGH, Thomas
    b. 30 Mar 1771, MacDonough, DE
    d. 23 May 1846, Middletown, DE
    Service: Commodore, Lake Champlain Squadron, on September 11, 1814 defeated
        British squadron under Commodore George Downie.
    Member - Clayton Cann Carter (collateral) [652/4112]

MACKENZIE, Thomas
    b. 20 Mar 1794, Calvert Co., MD
    d. 2 Jun 1866, Baltimore, MD
    Service: Private, Captain Kennedy's Company, 27th Rgt., Maryland Militia.
    Member - George Norbury Mackenzie [35/203]
        George Norbury Mackenzie, IV [369/1726]
        John Moores Maynadier Mackenzie [360/1699]

MACKUBIN, George
    b. 1789, Anne Arundel Co., MD
    d. 1853, Anne Arundel Co., MD
    m. Eleanor Mackubin, 26 Oct 1812, Anne Arundel Co., MD
    Service: Private, Artillery Company, 22nd Rgt., Maryland Militia.
    Member - William Joseph Lescure, 3rd [548/3099]

A CHRONICLE OF SOLDIERS, SEAMEN, AND MARINES

MAGEE, Alexander
    b. 20 Sep 1790, Philadelphia, PA
    d. 8 Jul 1845, New Bloomfield, PA
    m. Sarah Crever, Jan 1815, PA
    Service: Private, Captain William Alexander's Company, Pennsylvania Militia.
    Member - John Alexander Magee [560/3203]

MAGRUDER, Thomas
    b. 24 Nov 1779, Prince George's Co., MD
    d. 14 Aug 1830, Prince George's Co., MD
    m. Mary Clarke, 4 Jan 1808, Prince George's Co., MD
    Service: Quartermaster, 14th Rgt., Maryland Militia.
    Member - Caleb Clark Magruder, Jr. [263/1218]

MARTZ, George D.
    b. 31 May 1785, Frederick Co., MD
    d. 23 Feb 1868, Frederick Co., MD
    m. Catharine Reese, 23 Aug 1809, Frederick Co., MD
    Service: Captain, 16th Rgt., Maryland Militia.
    Member - Ralph Fraley Martz [622/3964]

MASSIE, John Witney
    b. 30 Oct 1790, Winchester, VA
    d. 1838, Alexandria, VA
    m. Mary Stuart Foote, 25 Feb 1824, Dumfries, VA
    Service: Private, 1st Rgt., Virginia Militia. 28 Aug 3 - Dec 1814.
    Member - Austin McCarthy McDonnell [236/1132]

MATHIOT, Jacob
    b. 14 Oct 1790, Lancaster, PA
    d. 10 May 1873, Columbia, PA
    m. Anna Nancy Wisler, Columbia, PA
    Service: Member of Captain James Clyde's "Columbia Independent Volunteers" attached to 49th Rgt., Maryland Militia at the Battle of Baltimore. 28 Aug - Sep 1814.
    Member - John Ward Willson Loose [656/2619]

A CHRONICLE OF SOLDIERS, SEAMEN, AND MARINES

MATTHEWS, William
    b. 2 Dec 1781, Charles Co., MD
    d. 19 Oct 1857, Charles Co. MD
    m. Mary M. Wheatly
    Service: Ensign, Captain Parnham's Company, 1st Rgt., Maryland Militia.
        18 Jul - 8 Aug 1814.
    Member - John Custis Handy [199/1002]

McCALL, William
    b. 20 Aug 1779, Mecklenburg Co., NC
    d. 28 Jul 1863, Gadsden Co., FL
    m. Parthena Vinson, 27 Apr 1799, Sumner Co., TN
    Service: Captain, 1st Rgt., Tennessee Militia.
    Member - Gary Edward Young [681/4359]

McCAULEY, James
    b.
    d. 13 Aug 1828, Cecil Co., MD
    m. Margaret S. Alexander, 29 Jul 1816, Cecil Co., MD
    Service: Private, 49th Rgt., Maryland Militia. 1 May 1813 - 27 Oct 1814.
    Member - Harold Kenneth Mackey [669/4213]

McCLAIN, John
    b. 1771, Scotland
    d. 15 Feb 1825, Baltimore, MD
    m. Elizabeth Holland, 6 Sep 1809, Baltimore, MD
    Service: Private, Captain Harris' Company, 1st Rgt., Maryland Militia.
        5 Aug 1813 - 30 Nov 1814.
    Member - Frank Mauldin McClain, Jr. [553/3146]

McCOMAS, Henry Gough
    b. 1795
    d. 12 Sep 1814, Baltimore Co., MD
    Service: Private, Captain Aisquith's Company, Sharp Shooters. Killed at the Battle
        of North Point.
    Member - Henry Clay McComas (collateral) [412/2209]

A CHRONICLE OF SOLDIERS, SEAMEN, AND MARINES

McCOMAS, Zaccheus Onion
    b. 31 Mar 1792, Baltimore, MD
    d. 13 May 1867, Hagerstown, MD
    m. Susan F. --
    Service: Private, Captain Lowrye's Company, 1st Rgt., Maryland Militia.
        24 Aug - 30 Oct 1814.
    Member - Henry Angle McComas [226/1075]
        Joseph Patton McComas [284/1393]

McCURLEY, Felix
    b. 25 Dec 1779, York Co., MD
    d. 12 Jun 1845, Baltimore, MD
    m. Mary Pierpoint, 13 Oct 1804, Baltimore, MD
    Service: Private, Captain Andrew Smith's Company, 51st Rgt., Maryland Militia.
        Aug - Oct 1814.
    Member - Felix McCurley [51/251]
        James Bernard McCurley, Sr. [613/3830]
        James Wallace McCurley [53/252]
        William Stran McCurley [375/1766]

McFERRAN, John
    b. 12 Oct 1793, Baltimore, MD
    d. 11 Aug 1868, Wheeling, WV
    m. Jean Bell
    Service: Sergeant, Captain Aisquith's Company of Rifleman, 1st Battalion, Mayland
        Militia. 19 Aug - 18 Oct 1814.
    Member - Allison Sweeney Fleming [191/972]

McGAW, John
    b. 27 Mar 1797, Harford Co., MD

    d. 24 Mar 1864, Harford Co., MD
    m. Mary Keen
    Service: 2nd Lieutenant, Captain Jenkins' Company of Cavalry, 7th Rgt.,
        Maryland Militia.
    Member - George Keen McGaw [233/1107]

A CHRONICLE OF SOLDIERS, SEAMEN, AND MARINES

McKEAN, James
    b. 24 Sep 1795, Washington Co., PA
    d. 1 Sep 1876, Scotch Grove, IA
    m. Nancy Smith, May 1822, Mercer Co., PA
    Service: Private, Captain Rea's Company, 135th Rgt., Pennsylvania Militia.
        2 Jan 1814 - 13 Feb 1814.
    Member - Stanley Lewis Howard [645/4027]

McLEAN, John, Jr.
    b. 15 Jan 1775, Albany, NY
    d. 22 Mar 1864, Walton, NY
    m. Ann Burnett, NY
    Service: Lieutenant, 5th Rgt., New York Militia.
    Member - John Lance Koenig [604/3627]

McMURRAY, Samuel
    b. 2 Oct 1792, Carroll Co., MD
    d. Oct 1850, Baltimore, MD
    m. Sarah Sillman
    Service: Sergeant, Captain Frizzell's Company, Nace's Rgt., Maryland Militia.
        1st Sergeant, Captain Murray's Company, 36th Rgt., Maryland Militia.
    Member - Ira Holden Houghton [207/1027]

McNEAL, James
    b. Mar 1777, Ireland
    d. 2 Aug 1857, Baltimore, MD
    m. Sarah Quinn
    Service: Private, Captain Brown's Company, 1st Rgt., Maryland Militia.
    Member - Joshua Vansant McNeal [142/693]

McPHERSON, Henry Hendley
    b. 1784, Charles Co., MD
    d. 24 Jul 1863, Washington, D.C.
    m. Elizabeth Hooten Stelle, 17 Sep 1816, Washington, D.C.
    Service: 2nd Lieutenant, Captain Stonestreet's Company, Newman's Rgt., Maryland
        Militia. 1 Feb - 1 May 1814.
    Member - Burton Francis Corson [624/1831]

A CHRONICLE OF SOLDIERS, SEAMEN, AND MARINES

McWILLIAMS, John
    b. 25 Mar 1781, Wallkill, NY
    d. 1 Jul 1850, Scotchtown, NY
    m. Nancy Stitt, 23 Dec 1802, Wallkill, NY
    Service: Private, New York Militia. 7 Sep 1814 - 8 Dec 1814.
    Member - Douglas Lyman McWilliams [713/4765]

MEDAIRY, John
    b. 25 Oct 1795, Reisterstown, MD
    d. 11 Sep 1857, Baltimore, MD
    m. Rachel Russell, 20 Jan 1820, Baltimore, MD
    Service: Private, Captain Adreon's Company, 5th Rgt., Maryland Militia.
    Member - Bernard John Medairy [562/3204]
        Bernard John Medairy, Jr. [554/3162]
        George R. Medairy [46/239]
        Jacob H. Medairy [47/247]

MEIGS, Luther
    b. 26 May 1792, St. Albans, VT
    d. 6 Feb 1865, Highgate, VT
    m. Phebe Stockwell
    Service: Private, Captain Wood's Company, Dixon's Rgt., Vermont Militia.
    Member - Henry Benjamin Meigs [165/877]

MERRIKEN, Joseph R.
    b.
    d.
    Service: Private, 3rd Company, 39th Rgt., Maryland Militia.
    Member - Robert E.L. Marr [55/195]
        William G. Marr [54/194]
        David Willis Merriken [16/177]

MERRITT, Benjamin
    b. 6 Oct 1779, Kent Co., MD
    d. 17 Mar 1833, Kent Co., MD
    m. Eliza Jane Black
    Service: Private, Captain Boyer's Detachment, 8th Rgt., Maryland Militia.
    Member - James Black Merritt, 3rd [171/925]

A CHRONICLE OF SOLDIERS, SEAMEN, AND MARINES

MERRYMAN, Nicholas Rogers
    b. 26 Apr 1788, Hereford, MD
    d. 21 Jan 1864, Hereford, MD
    m. Anna Marie Gott, 15 Sep 1823, Baltimore Co., MD
    Service: Cornet, Captain Bosley's Company, 6th Cavalry District, Maryland Militia. 30 Jul 1812. 2nd Lieutenant, Maryland Militia. 15 Dec 1814.
    Member - Nicholas Bosley Merryman of J. [742/4956]

MERWINE, Jacob
    b. 8 Apr 1785, Northampton Co., PA
    d. Northampton Co., PA
    Service: Private, Captain John Dornblazer's Company, 2nd Brigade, 2nd Division, Pennsylavania Militia. 21 Oct 1814.
    Member - Richard Carl Schlenker (collateral) [642/3986]

METCALFE, Thomas
    b. 5 February 1783, Frederick Co., MD
    d. 7 March 1862, Uniontown, MD
    m. Martha Hiteshew, 27 December 1810, Uniontown, MD
    Service: Private, Captain Durbin's Company, Maryland Militia. 24 August - 15 October 1814. Sergeant, Captain Cumming's Company, 14th Rgt., Maryland Militia. 15 October 1814 - 15 June 1815.
    Member - David F. Englar, Jr. [404/2080]
        Philip Myers [390/1886]
        Philip Myers, III [428/2298]

METTEE, Martin
    b. 27 Dec 1787, Baltimore, MD
    d. 25 Nov 1854, Baltimore, MD
    m. Elizabeth Rowe Howard, 8 Oct 1818, Baltimore, MD
    Service: Private, Captain Wilson's Company, 6th Rgt., Maryland Militia. 12 Sep 1814.
    Member - Bradley T.J. Mettee, Jr. [674/4291]

A CHRONICLE OF SOLDIERS, SEAMEN, AND MARINES

METZGER, Jacob
- b. 23 Dec 1798, E. Hempfield, PA
- d. 17 Mar 1843, W. Hempfield, PA
- m. Mary Smalling
- Service: Private, 124th Rgt., Pennsylvania Militia.
- **Member** - Fred J. Metzger [589/3480]

MIDDLETON, Richard
- b. 24 Nov 1786, Annapolis, MD
- d. 6 Oct 1869, Baltimore, MD
- m. Sarah Reynolds
- Service: Private, Independent Blues, 5th Rgt., Maryland Militia.
- **Member** - Charles England [176/936]

MILBOURNE, James
- b. circa 1790, MD
- d. between 1855/60, Somerset Co., MD
- m. Catherine Dickerson, 15 Jul 1823, Worcester Co., MD
- Service: Private, Captain Whittington Polk's Company, 1st Battalion, 23 Rgt., Maryland Militia. 14 Apr - May 15, 1814.
- **Member** - Willis Clayton Tull, Jr. [647/4080]

MILLER, Andrew
- b. 1 Jan 1777, Baltimore, MD
- d.
- m. Caroline Dawes
- Service: Private, Captain Jacob Deems' Company, 51st Rgt., Maryland Militia. Taken prisoner at Battle of North Point 12 September 1814. He was held at Barbadoes Islands until the end of the war.
- **Member** - Arthur D. Gaus [409/2165]
  - Lewis H. Miller [4/10]

MILLER, John
- b. 1791, Frederick Co., MD
- d. 1845, Westminster, MD
- m. Charity Hellfenstein
- Service: Volunteer, Captain Gregory's Company, 3rd Rgt., Virginia Militia. 19 Apr - 3 Aug 1814.
- **Member** - Charles Robert Miller [329/1539]

A CHRONICLE OF SOLDIERS, SEAMEN, AND MARINES

MILLS, Ezekiel
    b. 14 May 1757, Snow Hill, MD
    d. 15 July 1847, Baltimore, MD
    m. Mary Jane Sands, 19 October 1812, Baltimore, MD
    Service: Private, Baltimore Union Artillery, Captain John Montgomery's 1st Rgt., Maryland Militia.
    Member - Albert Hampson Dell [371/1730]
        Charles Squires Dell [362/1712]
        Samuel Mills Dell [363/1711]
        Thomas Medairy Dell [227/1076]
        Thomas Medairy Dell, Jr. [364/1713]
        Ezekiel Mills, Jr. [21/182]
        George Albert Mills [33/192]
        Rowland Tearley Mills [277/1341]

MILTENBERGER, Anthony Felix Wybert
    b. 18 Dec 1789, Baltimore, MD
    d. 21 Oct 1869, Baltimore, MD
    m. Dorothea A. Warner, 7 Nov 1811, Baltimore, MD
    Service: Captain, 38th Rgt., U. S. Infantry. 20 May 1813.
    Member - Miltenberger Hall Worthington, Jr. [511/2855]

MITCHELL, George Edward
    b. 3 Mar 1781, Elkton, MD
    d. 28 Jun 1832, Washington, D.C.
    m. Mary Hooper, 28 May 1816, Cambridge, MD
    Service: Appointed Major, 3rd Artillery, U.S. Army. 1 May 1812.
        Raised Company of Cecil Co. Volunteers - Summer 1812. Service at Albany, and Sackett's Harbor on Lake Ontario. Promoted Lieutenant Colonel - 3 Mar 1813. Breverted Colonel, 14 Aug 1814 for gallantry displayed at Oswego. Resigned 1 Jun 1821.
    Member - Robert Levis Mitchell [297/1456]
        William Arthur Mitchell [414/2213]

A CHRONICLE OF SOLDIERS, SEAMEN, AND MARINES

MOALE, Samuel
    b. 4 Jan 1773, Baltimore, MD
    d. 13 Feb 1857, Baltimore, MD
    m. Ann G. White
    Service: Captain, 3rd Brigade, of Maryland Militia.
    Member - John Foster Moale, Jr. [583/3445]
        John Gray Foster Moale, [503/2791]

MONMONIER, Francis
    b. 29 Sep 1790, Paris, France
    d. Jul 1876, Baltimore Co., MD
    m. Susanna Boyle
    Service: 2nd Sergeant, Fell's Point Rifleman, 1st Battalion Rifles, Maryland Militia.
    Member - Harry Culver Martin [121/535]

MOORE, Asa
    b. 29 Feb 1783, VA
    d. 1856, Webster Co., MO
    m. Rebecca --
    Service: Private, Captain Nathan Farmer's Company Mounted Rifleman, Tennessee Militia. 28 Jan - 10 May 1814
    Member - Richard Norvel Andriano-Moore [651/4084]

MORRIS, John B.
    b. 5 Oct 1785, Somerset Co., MD
    d. 24 Dec 1874, Baltimore, MD
    m. Ann Cottman, Snow Hill, MD
    Service: Major in the Defense of Baltimore served on the staff of Major General William Winder, his kinsman.
    Member - Maurice A. Harnett, III (collateral) [599/3581]

MOTT, Benjamin
    b. 1774, New Hanover, NC
    d. 17 Dec 1849, Wilmington, NC
    m. Mary McCullough
    Service: Private, Captain Moore's Company, North Carolina Militia.
    Member - Carl Francis Bessent [614/3831]

A CHRONICLE OF SOLDIERS, SEAMEN, AND MARINES

NEILSON, Robert
   b. 22 Feb 1792, Eney, Ireland
   d. 21 Jul 1845, Baltimore, MD
   m. Catharine Ellender, 7 Apr 1825, Baltimore, MD
   Service: Private, Captain Cock's Company, 27th Infantry, Maryland Militia.
   Member - Alexander Thompson Dukes [239/1135]
        George Peabody Neilson [156/772]
        Robert Musgrave Neilson [141/692]

NEVEN, Thomas Addison
   b. 1790, Belfast, Ireland
   d. Dec 1845, Baltimore, MD
   m. Elizabeth Scott
   Service: Private, 8th Company, 6th Rgt., Maryland Militia.
   Member - Samuel Addison Downs [6/12]
        Thomas Neven Green [50/250]

NEWMAN, Horatio
   b. 1783, Prince Georges Co., MD
   d. 12 Feb 1865, Prince Georges Co., MD
   m. Eliza Ann Alvey, 13 Jan 1813, Prince Georges Co., MD
   Service: Private, Captain Brooke's Company, 34th Rgt., Maryland Militia.
   Member - Harry Wright Newman [479/2626]

NICOLL, Thomas
   b.
   d. Oct 1894
   m. Sarah Brevard
   Service: Private, Fells' Point Rifles, 1st Rifle Battalion, Maryland Militia.
   Member - Benjamin Brevard Nicoll [30/187]

NIVIN, David
   b. 29 Mar 1764, Mill Creek Hundred, DE
   d. 15 Dec 1823, Mill Creek Hundred, DE
   m. Tabitha McMechen, 7 Jun 1792, Mill Creek Hundred, DE
   Service: Commanded Second Rgt., First Brigade, Delaware Militia.
        14 May 1810 - 18 Jun 1814.
   Member - George Reece Corey [730/4839]
        Roland Reece Corey, Jr. [690/4496]

A CHRONICLE OF SOLDIERS, SEAMEN, AND MARINES

NOEL, Jacob
    b. Alsace, France
    d. abt. 1821, Hanover, PA
    m. Elizabeth Kreidler, Hanover, PA
    Service: Private, Captain Spangler's, 5th Rgt., Maryland Militia.
    Member - Jacob Edmond Noel [124/560]

NORTON, Zacheus (Zachariah)
    b. 8 Feb 1790, Shenandoah Co., VA
    d. 4 Jun 1865, North Bristol, OH
    Service: Private, Captain Moses' Company, Ohio Militia. 24 Aug - 5 Sep 1812.
    Member - Richard Pearson Norton [378/1805]

NORWOOD, John
    b.
    d.
    m. Margaret Samuels
    Service: Private, 1st Company, 39th Rgt., Maryland Militia.
    Member - Randolph Norwood [65/302]

OBENSHAIN (Abendschon or Ovenshain), William
    b. 3 Jun 1780, Berkeley, VA
    d. 11 Jun 1854, Fincastle, VA
    m. Sarah Fester (Foster), 16 Feb 1813, Fincastle, VA
    Service: Private, Captain James Carymill's Company, 48th Rgt., Virginia Militia.
        12 Jul - 28 Sep 1813.
    Member - Robert Spencer Wood [700/4589]

OLIVER, John
    b. 17 Jan 1791, Harwich, MA
    d. 9 Nov 1879, Newstead Twp., NY
    m. Phoebe Dykins, Nov 1813, Orleans, NY
    Service: Private, Captain Freegift Tuthill's Company, New York Militia.
        8 Sep - 8 Dec 1814.
    Member - Ernest L. Snider [697/4460]

A CHRONICLE OF SOLDIERS, SEAMEN, AND MARINES

OWENS, James Jr.
    b. 8 Mar 1776, Anne Arundel Co., MD
    d. 4 Sep 1864, Anne Arundel Co., MD
    Service: Private, Captain Burke's Company, 6th Rgt., Maryland Militia.
        19 Aug - 18 Nov 1814.
    Member - Christian Emmerich Mears [351/1637]

OWENS, Joseph
    b. 4 February 1780, Anne Arundel Co., MD
    d. 15 January 1849, Anne Arundel Co., MD
    m. Ann Rutter, 17 April 1805
    Service: Private, Captain Sterett's Independent Company, Maryland Militia.
        Wounded at the Battle of North Point.
    Member - Edward Burneston Owens [138/687]
        Edward Burneston Owens, Jr. [333/1588]
        William Councilman Owens [426/2290]

OWENS, Joseph
    b. 1788, Anne Arundel Co., MD
    d. 1880, Crownsville, MD
    m. Sallie McCenie, 22 January 1817, Anne Arundel Co., MD
    Service: Captain, 5th U.S. Infantry. At the Battle of Erie taken prisoner of War and
        held for several weeks in 1814. 12 December 1808 - June 1815.
    Member - Arthur Cecil Bond [424/2274]

OWINGS, Thomas of Richard
    b. 30 Apr 1788, Baltimore Co., MD
    d. 19 Feb 1863, Anne Arundel Co., MD
    m. Ann Maria Warfield, 29 Mar 1824, Anne Arundel Co., MD
    Service: Private, Captain Simmons'Company, Maryland Militia.
        Enlisted 19 Aug 1814.
    Member - Ralph Allen Eastwood, Sr. [644/4041]

PADDISON, Samuel
    b. circa 1784, Talbot Co., MD
    d. Mar 1814, Talbot Co., MD
    Service: Staff Officer, 4th Rgt., Maryland Militia.
    Member - Joseph Elmer Weisheit, Sr. [465/2557]

A CHRONICLE OF SOLDIERS, SEAMEN, AND MARINES

PAGE, James
    b. 1783, Baltimore, MD
    d. 15 Mar 1832, Baltimore, MD
    m. Mariah Coulter
    Service: Surgeon, Baltimore Station, U.S. Navy. 7 Sep 1807 - 14 Jun 1824.
    Member - Albert Page Boyce [166/889]
              Heyward Easter Boyce [244/1150]

PARRISH, William
    b. 7 Feb 1794, Baltimore, MD
    d. 23 Sep 1833, Baltimore, MD
    m. Eliza Ball, 1 Nov 1816, Baltimore, MD
    Service: Private, Captain Aisquith's 1st Rifle Sharpshooters, Maryland Militia.
    Member - James Hagerty Parrish [83/383]
              William Tippett Parrish [84/384]
              John King Wetter [276/1316]

PECHIN, William
    b. 1773, Philadelphia, PA
    d. 1 Aug 1849, Philadelphia, PA
    Service: Major, 6th Rgt., Maryland Militia.
    Member - Edward Duncan Hyde [402/2078]

PENNINGTON, Fredus
    b. 9 Apr 1793
    d. 30 Nov 1856
    m. Elizabeth Van Heckel, 3 Sep 1819
    Service: 3rd Lieutenant, 15th Rgt., Maryland Militia.
    Member - Fredus Edmund Sutton [484/2656]

PENNINGTON, Josias
    b. 2 Jun 1797, Baltimore, MD
    d. 23 May 1874, Baltimore, MD
    m. Sophia Cook Clapham
    Service: Private, United Volunteers, 5th Rgt., Maryland Militia.
    Member - Josias Pennington [230/1096]

A CHRONICLE OF SOLDIERS, SEAMEN, AND MARINES

PENTZ, Daniel
    b. 2 Dec 1794, York, PA
    d. 15 Jan 1871, Baltimore, MD
    m. Martha Hair, 10 Jan 1833, Baltimore, MD
    Service: Private, Captain Piper's Company, United Military Artillery, Maryland Militia.
    Member - Irvin Holden [485/2657]
        Franklin Eldridge Pentz [158/826]
        William Fletcher Pentz [159/827]

PENTZ, John Joseph
    b. 3 May 1790, York, PA
    d. 9 June 1853, Baltimore, MD
    m. Barbara Gould, 27 September 1810, Baltimore, MD
    Service: Private, Baltimore Independent Blues, Maryland Militia.
    Member - Joseph Pentz Martin [429/2299]
        Benjamin Hayden Pentz [405/2081]
        John Angelo Pentz [388/1884]
        John Joseph Pentz [403/2079]

PERKINS, John
    b. 13 Nov 1780, Prince Georges Co., MD
    d. 8 Nov 1840, Prince Georges Co., MD
    m. Harriet Gorsuch, 12 May 1809, Baltimore Co., MD
    Service: Private, Baltimore United Volunteers, 5th Rgt., Maryland Militia.
        19 Aug - 18 Nov 1814.
    Member - Summerfield Davis Hall [238/1134]
        William Bartholow McDonald [179/946]
        William Henry Perkins, Jr. [237/1133]

PHILLIPS, Benjamin
    b. 1797, Dorchester Co., MD
    d. 1854, Dorchester Co., MD
    m. Mary Hooper, 9 Jan 1822, Dorchester Co., MD
    Service: Private, Captain John Travers' Company, 48th Rgt., Maryland Militia.
    Member - George Thomas Phillips [246/1152]
        George Thomas Phillips, Jr. [278/1361]
        Levi Benjamin Phillips [309/1497]
        Fletcher Phillips Williamson [607/3749]
        Jeffrey Phillips Williamson [649/4082]

A CHRONICLE OF SOLDIERS, SEAMEN, AND MARINES

PICKERING, Thomas
- b. 22 September 1791, Newington, NH
- d. 26 January 1871, Wood Co., VA
- m. Alomira K. Vaughn, 23 April 1844, Wood Co., VA
- Service: Served in Navy or possibly on a Privateer. Captured and imprisoned by the British. 12 Jul 1812 - 1813.
- **Member** - Barrett Lee McKown [738/4905]

PINKFIELD, Samuel
- b. circa 1775, Queen Anne's Co., MD
- d. circa 1829, Queen Anne's Co., MD
- m. Sarah Hye, 19 Apr 1808, Caroline Co., MD
- Service: Private, 38th Rgt., Maryland Militia. 10 May 1813 - 20 Sep 1814.
- **Member** - Nelson Franklin Faulkner, Jr. [704/4635]

PINKNEY, William
- b. 1764
- d. 1822
- Service: Major, 1st Rifle Battalion, Stricker's Brigade, 6th Rgt., Maryland Militia.
- **Member** - William Pinkney Whyte, Jr. [44/228]

POINDEXTER, Richard
- b. circa 1778-1780, Louisa Co., VA
- d. 13 Mar 1863, Louisa Co., VA
- m. Lucy T. Nelson, 20 Aug 1817, Louisa Co., VA
- Service: Private, Captain George Morris' Company, Virginia Militia. 28 Aug - 3 Dec 1814.
- **Member** - Cecil Miles Massie, Sr. [693/4494]

PORTER, Wrixham Lewis
- b. 7 Apr 1771, Somerset Co., Md
- d. 22 Oct 1816, Somerset Co., MD
- m. Priscilla Riggin, 30 Jul 1799, Somerset Co., MD
- Service: Private, Captain Heath's Company, 23rd Rgt., Maryland Militia.
- **Member** - Griffith Fontaine Pitcher [500/2767]
  William Henry Pitcher, Jr. [377/1768]

A CHRONICLE OF SOLDIERS, SEAMEN, AND MARINES

RABORG, Christopher, 2nd
    b. 6 Mar 1779, Baltimore, MD
    d. 13 Feb 1862, Baltimore, MD
    m. Ann Goddard, Mar 1805, Philadelphia, PA
    Service: Sergeant, Captain Sterett's Independent Company, 5th Rgt., Maryland Militia.
    Member - Edward Livingston Raborg [264/1221]

RAMSBURG, Frederick
    b. 18 Oct 1793, Frederick, MD
    d. 20 Jun 1836, Frederick, MD
    m. Lydia A. Snook, 21 May 1818, Frederick, MD
    Service: Private, Captain Nicholas Turnbull's Company, 1st Rgt., Camp Diehl, Maryland Militia. 2 Sep - 6 Nov 1814.
    Member - Charles Edward Kemp [708/4707]

RANDALL, Beale
    b. 1782, Baltimore Co., MD
    d. 1853, Baltimore Co., MD
    m. Martha Robinson
    Service: Major, 2nd and 15th Rgt., Maryland Militia. 8 Jul 1813 - 12 Nov 1814.
    Member - Watson Beale Randall [94/398]

RANDALL, Thomas
    b. 1792, Annapolis, MD
    d. 1877, Washington, D.C.
    m. Laura Wirt, 1830, Richmond, VA
    Service: Fought in the Battle of Bladensburg, wounded and captured by the British. He was sent to Canada and imprisoned until the war's end.
    Member - John LeMoyne Randall [655/4115]

RAWLINGS, Benjamin
    b. 1786, Annapolis, MD
    d. 1834, Baltimore, MD
    Service: 1st Lieutenant, Captain Schwarzouer's Company, 27th Rgt., Maryland Militia.
    Member - James Madison Rawlings [368/1725]

A CHRONICLE OF SOLDIERS, SEAMEN, AND MARINES

REED, Henry Ludovicus
    b. 18 Sep 1790, Weymouth, MA
    d. 16 Sep 1886, Chambersburg, PA
    m. Charlotte Stickney
    Service: Private, Captain John R. Jone's Company, Virginia Militia.
        Mar 18-29, 1813; Sep 20-30, 1814.
    Member - John Ludovicus Reed [103/416]

REEDER, Charles
    b. 8 Apr 1787, Bucks Co., PA
    d. 15 Apr 1855, Baltimore, MD
    m. Elizabeth Clark, Bucks Co., PA
    Service: Private, Captain Benjamiin Howard's Company, Maryland Militia.
        19 Aug - Nov 1814.
    Member - William Wallace Lanahan [335/1594]
        Edward McColgan [336/1595]
        Amos Alphonse Reeder, Jr. [353/1647]
        Charles Howard Reeder [337/1597]
        Charles Leonard Reeder [338/1597]
        Charles Merrick Reeder [334/1589]
        Charles Merrick Reeder, Jr. [358/1670]
        Clarence Reeder [347/1628]
        James Dawson Reeder [339/1598]
        Leonard Ben Reeder [340/1599]
        Maurice Lanahan Reeder [341/1600]
        Oliver H. Reeder [443/2324]
        Thomas Leonard Reeder [354/1648]
        Thomas Leonard Reeder, Jr. [662/4202]

REILLY, Patrick
    b. 1797, Co. Monaghan, Ireland
    d. 15 Jun 1847, Baltimore, MD
    m. Harriet Jones, Baltimore, MD
    Service: Private, Captain Brown's Eagle Artillery, Maryland Militia.
    Member - Clement Dumont Erhardt, Jr. [571/3273]
        Clement Dumont Erhardt, III [627/3960]

A CHRONICLE OF SOLDIERS, SEAMEN, AND MARINES

REIP, Henry
   b.
   d.
   Service: Private, Captain Philip B. Sadtler's Company, Baltimore Yeagers, 5th Rgt., Maryland Militia.
   Member - Alfred H. Reip [1/167]
             Thomas Henry Reip [23/169]

REYNOLDS, John
   b. Mar 1793, Queen Anne Co., MD
   d. Mar 1881, Washington, D.C.
   m. Ellen Dunn
   Service: Private, Captain Coat's Company, Maryland Militia.
   Member - Charles Ambrose Reynolds [69/322]
             William Butler Reynolds [126/583]

RICHARDSON, William Hervey
   b. 22 Feb 1790, Warren Co., VA
   d. 10 Apr 1853, Charleston, IL
   m. Susannah Wright Bowman, 3 Jan 1811, Shenandoah Co., VA
   Service - Lieutenant, Captain Edmund Taylor's Company, Mounted Rifelman, Virginia Militia.
   Member - Merrill Duane Berkeley [632/3987]

RIDGATE, Benjamin Cornick
   b. 21 Sep 1788, Port Tobacco, MD
   d. 5 Apr 1858, Washington, D.C.
   m. Margareth Elizabeth King
   Service: Private, 1st Baltimore Hussars, 5th Rgt., Maryland Militia.
   Member - Thomas Howe Ridgate [128/603]

RIEMAN, Henry
   b. 14 Dec 1786, Baltimore, MD
   d. 27 Apr 1865, Baltimore, MD
   m. Mary Jones
   Service: Private, Captains Hook's and Hunt's Companies, Maryland Militia.
   Member - Charles Ellet Rieman [441/2322]

A CHRONICLE OF SOLDIERS, SEAMEN, AND MARINES

RIGGS, Elisha
- b. 13 Jun 1779, Montgomery Co., MD
- d. 3 Aug 1853, New York, NY
- m. Alice Lawrason, 12 Sep 1812
- Service: Ensign, Captain Owing's Company, 32nd Rgt., Maryland Militia. Commissioned 23 Apr 1812. Private, Captain Rothrock's Company, 38th Rgt., U.S. Infantry, 4 Jun 1813 - 4 Jun 1814.
- **Member** - Clinton Levering Riggs [243/1149]
    Richard Cromwell Riggs [365/1714]

RIMMER, Thomas
- b. 1780, Granville Co., NC
- d. ca. 1845, Madison Co., IL
- m. Jemima Jacobs, 22 Jul 1800, Person Co., NC
- Service: Corporal in Captain George Dabney's Company, 43rd Rgt., North Carolina Militia. 25 Mar 1814 - 18 Feb 1815.
- **Member** - L.E. Kielman [698/4587]
    Toxie L. Kielman [712/4706]

ROBERTS John
- b. 3 Jun 1762, Dames Quarter, MD
- d. 27 Oct 1846, Dames Quarter, MD
- m. Martha Roberts, 28 Dec 1824, Dames Quarter, MD
- Service: Sergeant, Captain William White's Company, 23rd Rgt., Maryland Militia. 18 May 1814 - 7 Jun 1814.
- **Member** - John Drew Ford [727/4817]
    Mark Douglas Lederer Ford [737/4904]
    George Francis Sanders, III [468/2560]

ROBERTS, William
- b. Talbot Co., MD
- d. between 1814-1818, Baltimore, MD
- Service: 2nd Lieutenant, Captain Banning's Company, 9th Cavalry District, Maryland Militia.
- **Member** - Henry Roberts [406/2105]

A CHRONICLE OF SOLDIERS, SEAMEN, AND MARINES

ROBERTSON, Julius Caesar Nichols
    b. 20 Feb 1792, Jonesboro, TN
    d. 1 Jan 1880, Hernando, MS
    m. Margaret Reagan, 14 May 1818
    Service: Private, Captain Evan's Company, Tennessee Militia. Battle of New Orleans, 1815.
    Member - Carl Hoak Stewart, Jr. [520/2966]

ROLFE, Reuben
    B. circa 1780, Mecklenburg Co., VA
    d. circa 1830, Dinwiddie Co., VA
    m. Mary --
    Service: Corporal, 1st Rgt., Virginia Militia. 2 Aug 1814 - 4 Feb 1815.
    Member - Charles Irving Kratz, Jr. [707/4676]

ROLLE, Thomas
    b. 30 Jan 1794, Talbot Co., MD
    d. 3 Jan 1879, Talbot Co., MD
    m. Elizabeth H. Rolle, 24 Apr 1823, Talbot Co., MD
    Service: Private, Captain Joseph Kemp's Company, 26th Rgt., Maryland Militia. May 1813 - Sept 1814.
    Member - Joseph Howard Inloes [568/3272]

RONEY, William
    b. 26 Sep 1782, Belfast, Ireland
    d. 29 Dec 1844, Baltimore, MD
    m. Alice McBlair
    Service: Captain, 39th Rgt., Maryland Militia. 15 Jun 1813 - 1814.
    Member - Evan Warden Rinehart [190/968]
        Thomas Warden Rinehart [189/967]

ROSS, Reuben
    b. 1 Dec 1781, Baltimore, MD
    d. 9 Apr 1830, Baltimore, MD
    m. Sarah Shryer
    Service: 2nd Lieutenant, Baltimore Volunteer Artillery, 1st Rgt. Artillery, Maryland Militia.
    Member - Charles Thomas Holloway, II [279/1365]
        Reuben Ross Holloway [109/428]

A CHRONICLE OF SOLDIERS, SEAMEN, AND MARINES

ROTHROCK, John
   b. 27 Apr 1778, Baltimore, MD
   d. 14 Jul 1865, Baltimore, MD
   m. Margaret Agnew, 18 Mar 1860, Baltimore, MD
   Service: Captain, 38th U.S. Infantry. 20 May 1813.
   Member - John Lawson Bordley [461/2553]
            William Brown Hutchison [464/2556]

RUCKER, Richard
   b. Amherst Co., VA
   d. 1817
   m. Margaret Marr, 10 July 1798
   Service: Substitute for John Penn, Captain Cornelius Sale's Company, 8th Rgt., Virginia Militia. 5 months.
   Member - Guy Hudson Parr [433/2303]

RUSK, George
   b. 1790, Baltimore, MD
   d. 21 Mar 1838, Baltimore, MD
   m. Mary Krebs
   Service: Private, Fell's Point Light Dragoons, 5th Rgt. Calvary, Maryland Militia.
   Member - Jacob Krebs Rusk [145/712]

RUSSELL, Pliny
   b. 16 Oct 1787, Hadley, MA
   d. 7 Jul 1862, Northampton, MA
   m. Fanny Seymour, 13 Nov 1813, Greenfield, MA
   Service: Private, Captain David Stickland's Company, 5th Rgt., Masschusetts Militia. 13 Sep 1814 - 7 Nov 1814.
   Member - Richard Edward Anderson [732/4732]

RUST, Samuel
   b. 29 May 1781, MD
   d. 22 Feb 1863, Baltimore, MD
   m. Martha Dean
   Service: Private, Baltimore Independent Artillery, 1st Rgt., Maryland Militia.
   Member - James Knox Polk Boyd [167/899]

A CHRONICLE OF SOLDIERS, SEAMEN, AND MARINES

SADTLER, Philip Benjamin
    b. 16 Jun 1771, Homburg von der Hocke, Germany
    d. 3 Mar 1860, Baltimore, MD
    m. Catherine Captio Sauerwein, 8 Dec 1812, Baltimore, MD
    Service: Captain, Baltimore Yeagers, 5th Rgt., Maryland Militia. 22 Apr 1814.
    Member - Charles Herman Dickey [9/377]
        Edmund Sadtler Dickey [352/1646]
        Francis George Dickey [491/2731]
        Philip Sadtler Dickey [72/360]
        George Sadtler Robertson [245/1151]
        Charles Edward Sadtler [155/765]
        Charles Herbert Sadtler [37/207]
        Christopher Columbus Sadtler [64/306]
        Howard Plitt Sadtler [29/186]
        John Philip Benjamin Sadtler [75/334]

SAMBLE, (Sipley) Thomas
    b. 20 Feb 1783, Belgium
    d.
    m. Ann Maria von der Hoof
    Service: Seaman, Barney's Flotilla. 1814.
    Member - Samuel Henry Wade [89/393]

SANFORD, George
    b. 13 Dec 1770, Fairfax Co., VA
    d. 6 Aug 1837, Washington, D.C.
    m. Elizabeth Lowry, 11 Dec 1800
    Service: Corporal, Captain Buck's Company of Artillery, 2nd Rgt., Washington D.C. Militia. 19 Aug - 10 Sep 1814.
    Member - John Lowry Sanford [287/1407]

SAPPINGTON, Henry
    b. 1780, Anne Arundel Co., MD
    d.
    Service: Private, Captain Hammond's Company, Maryland Militia. 22 Aug - 24 Sep 1814.
    Member - Thomas Jonas Sappington [467/2559]

A CHRONICLE OF SOLDIERS, SEAMEN, AND MARINES

SCHMINKE, George
- b. 16 Jan 1776, Carlshaven, Hesse
- d. 16 Dec 1847, Baltimore, MD
- m. Ann Tschudy
- Service: Private, Baltimore Yeagers, 5th Rgt. Infantry, Maryland Militia.
- **Member** - Frederick William Schminke [27/170]

SCHOLL, Christian
- b. 1770, near Frederick, MD
- d. circa 1826, Frederick, MD
- m. Elizabeth Brunner
- Service: Private, Captain Getzendanner's Company, 16th Rgt., Maryland Militia.
- **Member** - Edward Derr Shriner, Jr. [506/2794]

SCHUCHTS, John Henry
- b. 1753, Berlin, Germany
- d. 4 May 1848, Baltimore Co., MD
- m. Mary Asher
- Service: Lieutenant Colonel, 2nd Rgt., Maryland Militia. 25 Jul - 11 Nov 1814.
- **Member** - John Henry Orem, Jr. [228/1086]

SEEGAR, Arthur
- b. circa 1792, Queen Anne's Co., MD
- d. Dec 1824, Queen Anne's Co., MD
- m. Frances H. Massey, 18 Jun 1818, Queen Anne's Co.
- Service: Private, Captain Joshua W. Massey's Company, 35th Rgt., Maryland Militia. Sep 12-23 1814.
- **Member** - John King Beck Emory Seegar, Jr. [721/4798]

SETH, James
- b. 2 Oct 1780, near Easton, MD
- d. 9 Oct 1829, Hebron, MD
- m. Sara Lambdin, 19 Sep 1802, Talbot Co., MD
- Service: Private, Captain John Carroll's Company, Maryland Militia.
- **Member** - Raymond B. Clark, Jr. [623/3882]

A CHRONICLE OF SOLDIERS, SEAMEN, AND MARINES

SHAFER, George
    b. 16 Mar 1787, Frederick, MD
    d. 9 Dec 1857, Frederick, MD
    m. Elizabeth Remsberg, 15 Feb 1812, Frederick, MD
    Service: Private, Captain George W. Ent's Company, 3rd Rgt., Hampstead Hill, Maryland Militia. 2 Sep - 6 Nov 1814.
    Member.- Charles Edward Kemp [708/4707]

SHANE, Daniel
    b. 1790
    d. 13 Jul 1824, Baltimore, MD
    Service: Private, Captain Shrim's Company, 5th Rgt., Maryland Militia. Wounded at Battle of North Point, 19 Aug - 18 Nov 1814.
    Member - Edward Milburn Shane [387/1880]

SHAW, Lemuel
    b. 1774, Cape May Co., NJ
    d. 1870, Montgomery Co., MD
    m. Rebecca Davis, 1796, Georgetown, D.C.
    Service: Artificer, 1st Rgt., District of Columbia Militia.
    Member - Gordon Malvern Fair Stick, Jr. [540/3067]

SHELDON, James
    b. Londonderry, Ireland
    d. Baltimore, MD
    m. Sarah Barnes
    Service: Private, Captain Chalmer's Company, 51st Rgt., Maryland Militia.
    Member - James Edward Byrd [213/1044]

SHIPLEY, Benjamin, Jr.
    b. 1775, Anne Arundel Co., MD
    d. Jul 1828, Anne Arundel Co., MD
    m. Amelia Webster, 16 Aug 1791, Baltimore Co., MD
    Service: Captain Henry Woodward's Company, 22nd Rgt., Maryland Militia. 28 Jul - 1 Sep 1813. John Hall's Company, 3rd Calvalry District, Maryland Militia. 23-30 Nov 1814.
    Member - William Charles Austin, Jr. [722/4799]

A CHRONICLE OF SOLDIERS, SEAMEN, AND MARINES

SHIPLEY, William
    b. 12 Sep 1777, New Castle Co., DE
    d. 17 Mar 1861, Baltimore, MD
    m. Ann Forrest
    Service: Captain, 4th Company, 1st Brigade, Delaware Militia. 25 Jul 1812.
    Member - John Guido Hisky [316/1509]
        Thomas Foley Hisky [232/1104]
        William George Hisky [317/1510]

SHOEMAKER, Robert
    b. 4 Oct 1782, Mohawk, NY
    d. 14 Apr 1838, Jolliet, IL
    m. Catherine Meyers
    Service: Major, New Jersey Militia.
    Member - Michael Meyers Shoemaker [110/429]

SLICER, Andrew
    b. 30 Nov 1774, Frederick, MD
    d. 20 Jun 1865, Annapolis, MD
    m. Elizabeth Selby, 29 Nov 1797, Annapolis, MD
    Service: Lieutenant, Captain Sand's Company, 22nd Rgt., Maryland Militia.
        20 Aug 1813. Captain, 42nd Rgt., Maryland Militia. 22 Apr 1814.
    Member - Edward Albert Rossmann [477/2614]

SLINGLUFF, Jesse
    b. 1 Jan 1775, Springfield Township, PA
    d. 30 Jun 1836, Frederick Co., MD
    m. Elizabeth Deardoff, 11 Sep 1799, Frederick Co., MD
    Service: Private, Captain Thompson's Company, 1st Baltimore Horse Artillery,
        Maryland Militia.
    Member - Francis Cross Marbury [680/4358]
        Jesse Slingluff, Jr. [407/2107]
        Michael McCormick Slingluff [682/4386]
        Robert Lee Slingluff [696/4286]

A CHRONICLE OF SOLDIERS, SEAMEN, AND MARINES

SLOAN, John
    b. 5 Aug 1777, Londonderry, Ireland
    d. 17 Aug 1829, Lexington, VA
    m. Mary Shields, 1804, Lexington, VA
    Service: Ensign, Captain McMullin's Company, 8th Rgt., Virginia Militia.
        29 Jul - 23 Sep 1814. Captain, 4th Rgt., Virginia Militia. 23 Sep 1814 - 18 Feb 1815.
    Member - Charles Wortham Sloan [268/1236]

SMICK, Peter
    b. circa 1790, Baltimore, MD
    d. 14 Oct 1813, Annapolis, MD
    m. Elizabeth Warner, 24 Dec 1805, Baltimore, MD
    Service: Private, Captain Slicer's Company, Maryland Militia. Died of Camp fever 14 Oct 1813.
    Member - Edward Graham Jones, Jr. [591/3549]
        Edward Graham Jones, III [608/3771]
        Beverly Polk Moore [621/3963]
        Christopher Polk Moore [630/3966]

SMITH, Benjamin B.
    b. 1786, Waterford, NY
    d. 1833, At Sea
    m. Ann Thompson
    Service: Private, Marine Artillery, Captain George Stiles' Company, Maryland Militia. 1814.
    Member - Asa H. Smith [34/193]
        Robert T. Smith [8/13]

SMITH, Sabritt
    b. 1775, Anne Arundel Co., MD
    d. 1830, Anne Arundel Co., MD
    m. Mary Hawkins, Apr 1798, Baltimore, MD
    Service: Private, Captain Abner Linthicum's Company, 22nd Rgt., Maryland Militia.
    Member - Richard Stewart Benson [590/3482]
        George Benson Keen [482/2651]

A CHRONICLE OF SOLDIERS, SEAMEN, AND MARINES

SMITHSON, Gabriel
   b. Harford Co., MD
   d. abt 1862, Baltimore, MD
   m. Ann Garner
   Service: Private, 40th Rgt., Maryland Miltia. 26 Apr - 4 May 1813.
   Member - John Henry Miller [229/1095]

SMULL, Jacob
   b. 1770, Baltimore, MD
   d. 12 Jul 1819, Baltimore, MD
   m. Elizabeth Luce, 25 Mar 1794, Baltimore, MD
   Service: Surgeon on the Privateer, *Jacob & Mary*. Oct 1812.
   Member - Ferdinand B. Focke [281/1375]
        Harry Smull Focke [327/1537]
        Walter David Focke [282/1376]
        William Focke Herman [416/2222]
        Richard Charles Manning, III [480/2639]
        George Warner Smull [393/1906]

SOLLIDAY, Jacob
   b. 2 Feb 1748, Bedminster Twp., PA
   d. 15 Apr 1815, Milford Twp., PA
   m. Barbara Loux, 20 Jun 1773, Bucks Co., PA
   Service: 1st Lieutenant, Captain Michael Petre's Company, Pennsylvania Militia.
       3 Sep 1814.
   Member - William Buchanan Gold, Jr. [617/2373]

SOULE, Howland
   b. 24 Mar 1793, Columbia Co., NY
   d.
   m. Sally Downing
   Service: Private, Captain Elting's Company, 3rd Rgt., New York Militia.
       14 Sep - 1 Nov 1814.
   Member - Arthur Van Horn [253/1167]

A CHRONICLE OF SOLDIERS, SEAMEN, AND MARINES

SPALDING, Joseph
    b. circa 1795, St. Mary's Co., MD
    d. IL
    m. Nancy Norris, circa 1812, St. Mary's Co., MD
    Service: Private, Captain Crouch's Company, 3rd Mounted Rgt., Kentucky Militia. 12 Oct 1812.
    Member - Crolian William Edelen [515/2859]

SPURRIER, Greenbury
    b. 3 Mar 1785, Frederick Co., MD
    d. 29 Dec 1866, Baltimore, MD
    m. Mary Shriner, 29 Aug 1811
    Service: Private, Captain Fonsten's Company, 3rd Rgt., Maryland Militia. 27 Oct 1814.
    Member - Oliver Walter Spurrier [512/2856]

STAIR (Stoehr), Daniel
    b. 14 May 1787, York Co., PA
    d. 29 Jul 1864, Hanover, PA
    m. Anna Eva Felty, 17 Nov 1814, Hanover, PA
    Service: Private, Captain Fred Metzger's Company, Pennsylvania Militia. Battle of North Point. 30 Aug - 25 Sep 1814.
    Member - William Stroman Stair, Jr. [743/4961]
             William Stroman Stair, Sr. [718/4770]

STALEY, Moses
    b. 11 Feb 1792, Frederick, MD
    d. 3 Jun 1841, Frederick, MD
    m. Ann Elizabeth Stull, 18 Sep 1816, Frederick, MD
    Service: Private, Captain Getzendanner's Company, 16th Rgt., Maryland Militia.
    Member - Charles Edward Kemp [708/4707]

STANSBURY, Elijah
    b. May 1791, Baltimore Co., MD
    d. 1883, Baltimore, MD
    m. Elizabeth Blizzard, Baltimore Co., MD
    Service: Private, Captain Montgomery's Company, Baltimore Union Artillery, Maryland Militia.
    Member - James Edward Stansbury (collateral) [440/2318]

A CHRONICLE OF SOLDIERS, SEAMEN, AND MARINES

STARR, William
- b. 1778, Baltimore, MD
- d. 4 Jul 1819, Baltimore, MD
- m. Rebecca McGlathery
- Service: Private, Captain Magruder's Company, 1st Rgt., Maryland Militia.
- **Member** - William Lamping [71/333]

STEINER, Henry
- b. 23 Jun 1775, Frederick, MD
- d. 18 May 1825, Frederick, MD
- m. Rachel Rebecca Murray
- Service: Captain, Steiner's Artillery, 1st Rgt., Maryland Militia.
- **Member** - Michael Meyers Shoemaker [110/429]

STEINER, Stephen
- b. 1767
- d. 1829
- m. Eliza Bausman
- Service: Captain, 16th Rgt., Maryland Militia. Promoted to Major 1 Aug 1814.
- **Member** - Edward E. Steiner [636/4006]

STEUART, George H.
- b.
- d. Oct 1867, Baltimore, MD
- m. Ann Jane Edmondson
- Service: Captain, 5th Rgt., Maryland Militia.
- **Member** - James Edmondson Steuart [125/582]

STEUART, William
- b. 1780, Baltimore, MD
- d. 12 Feb 1830, Baltimore, MD
- m. Elizabeth Hagerty
- Service: Lieutenant Colonel, 38th U.S. Infantry. 19 May 1813 - 15 Jun 1815.
- **Member** - Edwin Steuart Vaughan (collateral) [542/3084]

A CHRONICLE OF SOLDIERS, SEAMEN, AND MARINES

STEWART, John I.
  b.
  d. 10 Jan 1843, Baltimore, MD
  m. Mary E. Frazier, 31 Dec 1807, Dorchester Co., MD
  Service: Purser's Steward, Barney's Flotilla, U.S. Navy. 10 Mar - 28 Dec 1814.
  Member - Arthur John Pritchard [215/1049]

STEWART, Thomas
  b. 19 Oct 1783, Baltimore, MD
  d. 22 Oct 1833, Baltimore, MD
  m. Sarah --
  Service: Private, Baltimore Union Artilery, 1st Rgt., Maryland Militia.
  Member - John Thomas Deal, Jr. [13/175]

STICKNEY, Henry
  b. 21 Jul 1782, Boston, MA
  d. 1 May 1862, Mobile, AL
  m. Lydia Wells
  Service: Private, Baltimore Fencibles, 1st Rgt. Artillery, Maryland Militia.
  Member - George Henry Stickney [70/366]

STIFF, James
  b. Middlesex Co., VA
  d. Middlesex Co., VA
  Service: Sergeant, Captain Blake's Company, 109th Rgt., Virginia Militia.
      11 May 1813 - 11 Dec 1814.
  Member - Ashby Gordon Stiff, Jr. (collateral) [470/2575]

STIFF, William Nelson
  b. 30 Jan 1770, Middlesex Co., VA
  d. Middlesex Co., VA
  m. Sarah Healy, 28 Jan 1796, Middlesex Co., VA
  Service: Private, Captain Blake's Company, 109th Rgt., Virginia Militia.
      3 Apr 1813 - 26 Dec 1814.
  Member - Ashby Gordon Stiff [437/2308]

A CHRONICLE OF SOLDIERS, SEAMEN, AND MARINES

STOCKTON, John Cox
    b. 20 Nov 1786, Trenton, NJ
    d. 1869, Mt. Vernon, OH
    m. Ann Stillwell, 30 Mar 1811, Muskingum Co., OH
    Service: Quartermaster, McConnel's Rgt., Ohio Militia. 26 Aug - 9 Sep 1812.
    Member - James Howard Huddleson, Jr. [240/1142]

STONE, William
    b. 11 Sep 1739, Bermuda
    d. 8 Oct 1831, Baltimore Co., MD
    m. Hannah (Owings) Cockey, 20 Apr 1778, Baltimore Co., MD
    Service: Commanded Artillery at Battle of North Point.
    Member - John William Middendorf, Jr. [462/2554]

STREETT, John
    b. 1762, Harford Co., MD
    d. 7 May 1836, Harford Co., MD
    m. Martha St. Clair, 1786, Harford Co., MD
    Service: Lieutenant Colonel, 7th Rgt., Maryland Militia. 13 Feb 1812.
    Member - S.K. Fendall Waters [531/2998]

STRIBLING, Erasmus
    b. 1 Jun 1784, Hoepwell, VA
    d. 2 Jul 1858, Mason Co., VA
    m. Matilda Kinney
    Service: Captain of Artillery, Virginia Militia.
    Member - William Dewey Cooke [1897/965]

STROBEL, John Peter
    b. 16 Dec 1777, Hersbruckt, Germany
    d. 16 Feb 1859, Baltimore, MD
    m. Barbara Barder
    Service: Corporal, Eagle Artillerists, 1st Rgt., Maryland Militia.
    Member - Albert Perrigo Strobel [82/380]
        James William Strobel [214/1045]

A CHRONICLE OF SOLDIERS, SEAMEN, AND MARINES

SUMNER, Henry Payson
    b. 30 Aug 1787, Roxbury, MA
    d. 15 Feb 1839, Baltimore, MD
    m. Frances Allanly Steele
    Service: 3rd Sergeant, Independent Company, 5th Rgt., Maryland Militia.
    Member - William Henry Sumner [163/856]

SUMWALT, John T.
    b. 6 Jan 1791, Baltimore, MD
    d. 20 Aug 1868, Baltimore, MD
    m. Rachel Sparks
    Service: 4th Corporal, 1st Rgt., Maryland Militia. Fort McHenry Gun Battery 6, wounded during engagement. Sep 12-13, 1814.
    Member - John Edward Hough [25/185]
        Pliny Miles Hough [133/645]

SWISHER, John
    b. 23 Sep 1782, Sussex Co., NJ
    d. 1 Feb 1861, Franklin Co., OH
    m. Mary Peterson, 12 Sep 1802, Sussex Co., NJ
    Service: Private, Captain Robert Reed's Company, Ohio Militia. 28 Jul - Sep 1813.
    Member - John Davis Newell [688/4492]

TALBOTT, Richard
    b. abt. 1785, Anne Arundel Co, MD
    d. abt. 1840, Charles Co., MD
    m. Sarah A. Fainoll
    Service: Ensign, Captain Dorsey's Company of Cadets, 32nd Rgt., Maryland Militia.
    Member - Hattersly Worthington Talbott [139/691]
        Hattersly Worthington Talbott, Jr. [160/839]
        Otho Hollands Williams Talbott [161/838]

TAWS, Kenny (McKenna)
    b. Lawsonia, MD
    d.
    m. Nancy Nelson, 6 Aug 1819, Somerset Co., MD
    Service: Private, Captain William Juett, Maryland Militia. May 1813.
    Member - Thomas King Nelson Sterling [628/3970]

A CHRONICLE OF SOLDIERS, SEAMEN, AND MARINES

TAYLOR, John Bradford
    b. 2 Sep 1786, Baltimore, MD
    d. Jun 1864, Tallahassee, FL
    m. Mary Loockerman Chandler, 1845, Tallahassee, FL
    Service: Surgeon's Mate, 5th Rgt., Maryland Militia.
    Member - James Lookerman Taylor [286/85]

TAYLOR, Lemuel Greenberry
    b. 14 Feb 1791, Annapolis, MD
    d. 10 May 1859, Annapolis, MD
    m. Diademia Davis, 26 Apr 1809, Baltimore, MD
    Service: Captain, 5th Calvary, Maryland Militia. Battle of North Point.
    Member - Frank Paull Mitchell, Jr. [641/3770]
        Watson Beale Randall [94/398]

TAYLOR, Robert
    b. 2 Sep 1782, Baltimore, MD
    d. 16 Sep 1869, Baltimore, MD
    m. Elizabeth Stevenson, 25 Dec 1804, Baltimore, MD
    Service: Private, Captain Pennington's Company, Baltimore Independent Artillery. Maryland Militia.
    Member - Benjamin Franklin Taylor [175/935]
        Howard Richards Taylor [474/2600]

TAYLOR, William
    b.
    d.
    Service: Private, 4th Company, 27th Rgt, Maryland Militia.
    Member - Clifford Taylor [9/173]

TEALE, John Cranmer
    b. Leeds, England
    d. NY
    m. Grace Popham
    Service: Private, Captain Marsten's Company, 9th Rgt., New York Militia. 15 Sep - 15 Dec 1812.
    Member - Charles Edward Teale [152/747]

A CHRONICLE OF SOLDIERS, SEAMEN, AND MARINES

THOMAS, Sterling
   b. 14 Oct 1790, Baltimore, MD
   d. 11 Jan 1865, Baltimore, MD
   m. Elizabeth --, 1851
   Service: 4th Corporal, Captain James Foster's Company, 51st Rgt., Maryland Militia.
   Member - Robert Thomas Regester [593/3559]

THOMPSON, Henry
   b. 23 Jun 1774, Yorkshire, England
   d. 24 Aug 1837, Baltimore Co., MD
   m. Ann Lux Bowly, 29 Mar 1798, Baltimore Co., MD
   Service: Captain, Company of Cavalry, Maryland Militia.
   Member - Henry Oliver Thompson [285/1394]

THROCKMORTON, Josiah
   b. Henrico Co., VA
   d. 1833, Henrico Co., VA
   m. Sarah Williams Rahute
   Service: Private, Captain Friend's Company, 33rd Rgt., Virginia Militia.
      Mar 19-29, 1813.
   Member - Charles Woodson Throckmorton [198/998]

TODD, Bernard
   b.
   d. 1816
   m. May Green
   Service: Private, Captain Stansbury's Company, 6th Rgt., Maryland Militia.
      31 Aug - 18 Sep 1814.
   Member - Raymond Webb Thompson [271/1263]

TOZIER, Stephen
   b. 1790, Waterville, ME
   d. 8 Nov 1879, Waterville, ME
   m. Joanna Bates, 27 Aug 1818, Waterville, ME
   Service: Massachusetts Militia. 1814.
   Member - Herbert Leon Jenness [386/1867]

A CHRONICLE OF SOLDIERS, SEAMEN, AND MARINES

TROUT, Joseph
   b. 16 Oct 1787, Newtown, VA
   d. 26 Mar 1850, Port Republic, VA
   m. Sarah Whitesides
   Service: Private, Captain Sower's Company, Virginia Militia.
      4 Jan - 13 April 1814.
   Member - William Dewey Cooke [187/965]

TROVINGER, Joseph
   b. 11 Dec 1790, Washington Co., MD
   d. 11 May 1851, Washington Co., MD
   m. Elizabeth Clopper, 9 May 1822, Washington Co., MD
   Service: Private, Captain Cushwa's Company, Maryland Militia.
      27 Aug - 30 Oct 1814.
   Member - Tom Niel Rasmussen [715/4767]

TSCHUDY, Samuel
   b. 12 Feb 1788, Baltimore Co., MD
   d. 30 Apr 1868, Baltimore Co., MD
   m. Elizabeth Clem, 20 Mar 1817, Baltimore, MD
   Service: Private, Captain Sterretts Company, 1st Baltimore Hussars,
      Maryland Militia.
   Member - Harold Tschudi [312/1502]
      Samuel Werner Tschudi [299/1468]

TULL, John Nicholas
   b. 1771/75, Stokes Co., NC
   d. circa 1861, Henderson Co., TN
   m. Susan Baugh, circa 1800, Stokes Co., NC
   Service: Private, Captain Frederick Stunp's Company, Tennessee Militia.
      24 Sep - 10 Dec 1813.
   Member - John Earle Tull, Jr. [706/4703]

TURNER, Nathan
   b. 1773 or 1774, Baltimore Co., MD
   d. after 24 Mar 1855
   m. Elizabeth Fitch, 3 Feb 1796, Baltimore Co., MD
   Service: Private, Captain Magruder's Company, American Artillerists,
      Maryland Militia. Aug - Dec 1814.
   Member - Richard Nicolai Hambleton [508/2852]

A CHRONICLE OF SOLDIERS, SEAMEN, AND MARINES

VAN DEMAN, Henry
    b. 1789, OH
    d. 1872, Delaware, OH
    m. Sarah Darlington
    Service: Private, Captain Hamphill's Company, Col. McDonald's Rgt., Ohio Militia. 11 Aug - 3 Sep 1813.
    Member - William Henry Maltbie [221/1062]

VICKERS, Clement
    b. 7 Jan 1774, Dorchester Co., MD
    d. Talbot Co., MD
    Service: 1st Lieutenant, Captain Thomas' Company of Artillery, Maryland Militia. 24 Aug - 10 Sep 1814.
    Member - Robert Leonard Roberts [413/2212]
                Robert Leonard Roberts, Jr. [415/2221]

VICKERS, Joel
    b. 14 Aug 1774, Cecil Co., MD
    d. 2 Dec 1860, Baltimore, MD
    m. Ada Beck
    Service: 2nd Lieutenant, Marine Artillery, Maryland Militia.
    Member - William Handy Collins Vickers [136/674]

WALLS, Isaac
    b. 1773, Belfast, Ireland
    d. 4 Nov 1839, PA
    m. Mary Shepley
    Service: Served in War of 1812.
    Member - John Abbet Walls [469/2574]

WADDELL, Lyttleton
    b. 19 Oct 1790, Augusta Co., VA
    d. 11 Mar 1869, Staunton, VA
    m. Elizabeth Edmondson
    Service: Private, Lieutenant Crawford's Company, 5th Rgt., Virginia Militia.
    Member - William Dewey Cooke [187/965]

A CHRONICLE OF SOLDIERS, SEAMEN, AND MARINES

WARING, Francis
    b. Prince George's Co., MD
    d. abt. 1791-2, Anne Arundel Co., MD
    m. Elizabeth Turner
    Service: 3rd Sergeant, Captain Isaacs' Detachment, 34th Rgt., Maryland Militia.
    Member - Richard Mareen Duvall [210/1037]

WARING, John
    b. 1787, Essex Co., VA
    d. 10 Sep 1857, Essex Co., VA
    m. Elizabeth Latane, 10 Dec 1810, Essex Co., VA
    Service: Private, Captain Benjamin Fisher's Company, 6th Rgt., Virginia Militia. 1813-1814.
    Member - William Hunter Waring [566/3257]

WARNER, Andrew
    b.
    d.
    Service: Captain, 5th Company, 39th Rgt., Maryland Militia.
    Member - George E. Warner [39/209]
        John Edwin Warner [15/171]

WARNER, Michael
    b. 19 Sep 1774 Baltimore, MD
    d. 31 May 1848 Baltimore, MD
    m. Marie Elizabeth Beckley
    Service: Quartermaster, 51st Rgt., Maryland Militia.
    Member - John Lowry Sanford [287/1407]
        William Lanahan Sanford [398/2048]
        Culbreth Hopewell Warner [68/321]

WATERS, Richard Rawlings
    b. 14 Dec 1795, Montgomery Co., MD
    d. 5 Jan 1885, Montgomery Co., MD
    m. Jerusha Anne Shaw, 16 Dec 1817, Georgetown, D.C.
    Service: Private, Colonels Hood's and Bell's Rgt., Maryland Militia. 1 Aug - 27 Sep 1814.
    Member - Thomas Howard Fitchett Stick [539/3065]

A CHRONICLE OF SOLDIERS, SEAMEN, AND MARINES

WATERS, Zebulon
    b. 11 Sep 1784, Prince Georges Co., MD
    d. 28 Jan 1869, Baltimore, MD
    Service: Private, Captain Steuarts's Company, Washington Blues, Maryland Militia.
    Member - William Zebulon White (collateral) [510/2853]

WATKINS, Gassaway
    b. abt. 1752, Anne Arundel Co., MD
    d. 14 Jul 1840, Anne Arundel Co., MD
    m. Eleanor Bowie Claggett, 26 Apr 1803, Anne Arundel Co., MD
    Service: Lt. Colonel in Command of Troops at Annapolis, MD. 1813.
    Member - William Watkins Kenly [170/924]
        Edwin Warfield [88/390]

WATKINS, John
    b. 24 Aug 1782, Browningsville, MD
    d. 29 Sep 1866, Kemptown, MD
    m. Elenore C. Hitchcock, 8 Dec 1829, Frederick Co., MD
    Service: Private, Lieutenant Turbey F. Thomas' Detachment, 2nd Rgt., U.S. Infantry.
        3 Apr 1814 - 9 Apr 1815.
    Member - Robert Ellsworth Lyons [703/4634]

WATSON, Thomas
    b. Baltimore, MD
    d. Mar 1864, TX
    m. Rebecca Freeman
    Service: Captain, 3rd Company, 39th Rgt., Maryland Militia.
    Member - Watson Beale Randall [94/398]

WATTS, Nathaniel
    b.
    d.
    Service: Private, Captain A. Showers' Company, 15th Rgt., Maryland Militia. 1814.
    Member - Benjamin Watts [24/187]

A CHRONICLE OF SOLDIERS, SEAMEN, AND MARINES

WATTS, Thomas B.
   b.
   d.
   Service: Private, Sharp Shooters, 1st Rifle Batallion, Maryland Militia.
   Member - Frank L. Morling [14/176]

WEAVER, John
   b.
   d.
   m. Sarah Gorrich
   Service: Ensign, 1st Baltimore Light Infantry, Maryland Miltia.
   Member - John C. Bransby [76/362]

WEBB, Abner Jr.
   b. 5 Mar 1783, Scotland
   d. 28 Dec 1882, Baltimore, MD
   Service: Private, Captain Rogers' Company, 51st Rgt., Maryland Militia.
   Member - William Rollins Webb [342/1601]
          William Rollins Webb, Jr. [385/1862]

WEBB, William
   b. Kent Co, MD
   d. 22 Oct 1864, Chestertown, MD
   m. Mary Clough (Clow), 28 Aug 1825, Kent Co., MD
   Service: Private, Captain Foreman's Company, Maryland Militia.
       12 Sep - 23 Sep 1814.
   Member - Samuel Vannort Chapman [573/3280]
          Edward Trenholm Gieske, Jr. [596/3566]
          James Chapman Gieske [602/3689]

WEBSTER, John Adams
   b. 19 September 1787, Harford Co., MD
   d. 6 April 1875, Wilmington, DE
   m. Rachel Biays, 20 June 1821
   Service: 3rd Lieutenant, Privateer, *Rosse.* Sailing Master, Barney's Flotilla.
       Battle of Bladensburg. Fort McHenry in charge of six-gun battery, Ferry
       Branch.
   Member - Benjamin Bissell [256/1177]
          Charles Howard Tinges [419/2238]

A CHRONICLE OF SOLDIERS, SEAMEN, AND MARINES

WEIGLE, Samuel
    b. 1786, Hanover, PA
    d. 1864, MD
    m. Margarette Schaeffer, Hanover, PA
    Service: Private, Captain Bairs' Company, Pennsylvania Militia.
    Member - Howard Edward Young [346/1627]

WELLS, William
    b. 1763, KY
    d. 15 Aug 1812, Ft. Dearborn Massacre
    Service: Captain, Chief of Indian Scouts, General Harrison's command.
    Member - Rudolph A.A. Douglass [400/2071]

WELSH, William [74/361]
    b. 23 Jan 1800
    d. 1 Jun 1894
    m. Sarah Meriken
    Service: Private, Captain Levering's Company, Independent Blues, 5th Rgt., Maryland Militia.

WHELAN, Thomas
    b. 1776, Baltimore, MD
    d. 15 August 1859, Baltimore, MD
    m. Elisa Gegan
    Service: Private, Captain Leverings's Company, Independent Blues, 5th Rgt., Maryland Militia. 24 August - 18 November 1814.
    Member - Thomas Augustine Whelan [421/2253]

WHITEFORD, Hugh Jr.
    b. Harford Co., MD
    d. 25 Nov 1814, Harford Co., MD
    m. Eliza Doogan, 20 Mar 1804
    Service: Surgeon, Extra Battalion, Maryland Militia.
    Member - Roger Streett Whiteford, Jr. [501/2789]

A CHRONICLE OF SOLDIERS, SEAMEN, AND MARINES

WIEGAND, Daniel
    b. Apr 1793, Alsbach, Saxony, Germany
    d. 8 Aug 1839, Baltimore, MD
    m. Catherine Shriver, 26 Jun 1812, Baltimore, MD
    Service: Private, Captain Bader's Company, Union Yeagars, 1st Rifle Battalion, Maryland Militia. Battles of Bladensburg and North Point.
    Member - William Edward Wiegand [303/1489]
        William Green Wiegand [324/1528]

WILEY, John
    b. 30 Mar 1790, Norrisville, MD
    d. 17 Jan 1868, Norrisville, MD
    m. Elizabeth Ann Hutchins, 8 Dec 1826, Baltimore Co., MD
    Service: Private, Captain Benjamin Thomas' Company, 49th Rgt., Maryland Militia. 18 Apr - 16 May 1813. Private, Captain John Turner's Company, 42nd Rgt., Maryland Militia. 28 Aug - 26 Sep 1814. Private, Captain John Smithson's Company, 40th Rgt., Maryland Militia. 21-27 Oct 1814.
    Member - Ralph Wiley Sloan [664/4204]
        William Richard Wiley, Jr. [699/4588]

WILKINSON, Samuel
    b. 13 Aug 1794, Baltimore Co., MD
    d. 6 Aug 1868, Baltimore, MD
    m. Susannah Clark, 10 Aug 1839, Baltimore Co., MD
    Service: Private, Captain Stiles' Company, Marine Artillery, Maryland Militia.
    Member - Charles Marion Wilkinson [306/1493]

WILLIAMS, Joseph
    b. 1776
    d. abt 1852, nr. Middletown, DE
    m. Comfort Deputy
    Service: 1st Sergeant, Captain Ennis' Company, 7th Rgt., Delaware Militia.
    Member - George Washington Williams [325/1529]

A CHRONICLE OF SOLDIERS, SEAMEN, AND MARINES

WILLIAMS, Otho Holland
    b. 1784, Washington Co., MD
    d. Jul 1852, Washington Co., MD
    m. Elizabeth Bowie Hall
    Service: Major, Colonel Tilghman's Calvary at Bladensburg.
    Member - Hattersly Worthington Talbott, Jr. [160/839]

WILLIAMSON, James
    b. circa 1745-6, NJ
    d. circa Apr 1828, Mansfield Township, NJ
    m. Sarah Smith, circa 1763-65, NJ
    Service: Captain, New Jersey Militia. 17 Aug - 25 Sep 1812.
    Member - William Curtis Carroll Davis [495/2764]

WILLINGHAM, James
    b. 1785, St. Mary's Co., MD
    d. 18 Nov 1843, Baltimore, MD
    m. Sarah Garmin, 15 Jul 1815, Baltimore, MD
    Service: Private, Captain Peter's Company, 51st Rgt., Maryland Militia.
    Member - Daniel Francis Xavier Whiteford [563/3215]
          Lingard Ignatius Whiteford [575/3335]
          Lingard Ignatius Whiteford, Jr. [588/3481]

WILLIS, John
    b. 1765
    d. Apr 1839, Oxford, MD
    m. Margaret --
    Service: Lieutenant, Captain Eccleston's Detachment, Republican Blues, 11th Rgt., Maryland Militia. 23 September 1814.
    Member - Willliam Nicholas Willis [164/876]

WILSON, James
    b. 13 Sep 1792, Baltimore, MD
    d. 8 Feb 1880, Baltimore, MD
    m. Elizabeth Thorp
    Service: Sergeant, 3rd Company, 39th Rgt., Maryland Militia.
    Member - John James Wilson [99/391]

A CHRONICLE OF SOLDIERS, SEAMEN, AND MARINES

WILSON, John Sanford
    b. 15 Sep 1786, NJ
    d. 22 Aug 1881, Baltimore Co., MD
    m. Nancy Lemon
    Service: Private, Captain Snowden's Company, Maryland Militia.
    Member - John Sanford Wilson [122/557]

WILSON, Nicholas
    b. 176-?, MD
    d. Feb 1815, Baltimore Co., MD
    m. Sarah --
    Service: Private, Captain Charles Pumphrey's Detachment, 22nd Rgt.,
        Maryland Militia. 12 Apr - 24 Aug 1813. Private, Captain Henry Fowler's
        Company of Rifleman, Maryland Militia. 26 Aug 1814. Taken prisoner
        13 Sep 1814, sent to Halifax and died soon after return.
    Member - Henry Wilson Maglidt [678/4356]

WILSON, Thomas
    b. 27 Aug 1777, Baltimore, MD
    d. 12 Feb 1845, Baltimore, MD
    m. Mary Cruse
    Service: Private, Baltimore Independent Blues, 5th Rgt., Maryland Militia.
    Member - James Teackle Dennis [104/417]
        John Appleton Wilson [67/308]

WOOD, John
    b. abt. 1785, London, England
    d. abt. 1824, Baltimore, MD
    m. Charlotte Abbott
    Service: Private, Captain John Berry's Company, Washington Artillery, 1st Rgt.,
        Maryland Militia.
    Member - Philip Bryson Wood [105/418]

WOOD, Matthew
    b. circa 1780, Warwick Co., VA
    d. 1825, Warwick Co., VA
    Service: Private, in Captain John B. Cooper's Company, Virginia Militia.
        8 Feb - 11 Aug 1813.
    Member - Robert Emory Michel (collateral) [552/3138]

A CHRONICLE OF SOLDIERS, SEAMEN, AND MARINES

WOODRUFF, Joseph
    b. 12 Dec 1787, McIntosh, GA
    d. 12 Oct 1828, Charleston, SC
    m. Jane Campbell Harris, 8 Feb 1816, Charleston, SC
    Service: Major, 3rd U.S. Infantry. 12 Dec 1808 - 31 May 1822.
    Member - Caldwell Woodruff [274/1314]

WOODWARD, Philemon, Jr.
    b. 1778, New Kent Co., VA
    d. 9 Jun 1836, Middlesex Co., VA
    m. Elizabeth Roane Brockenborough, 8 Jul 1802, Richmond Co., VA
    Serivce: Sergeant-Major, Captain William L. Montague's Company, 109th Rgt., Virginia Militia.
    Member - William Fleming Parrish [551/3129]

WORLEY, Elijah
    b. 23 Jun 1788, Cerro Gordo, NC
    d. 1867, Cerro Gordo, NC
    Service: North Carolina Militia.
    Member - Aubrey DeVaughn Richardson (Collateral) [657/4292]

WORTHINGTON, Rezin Hammond
    b. 28 Jun 1794, Baltimore Co., MD
    d. 22 Jun 1884, Baltimore Co., MD
    m. Rachel Owings Shipley, 14 Jan 1823
    Service: Private, At the Battle of North Point.
    Member - Thomas Worthington Hollyday [373/1729]
        Richard Walker Worthington [289/1421]
        Thomas Chew Worthington [288/1418]
        Thomas Chew Worthington [301/1475]

WRIGHT, Alpha
    b. 26 Dec 1788, Litchfield Co., CT
    d. 1 Mar 1856, Tallmadge, OH
    m. Lucy Foster
    Service: Sergeant, Captain McArthur's Company of Rifleman, Ohio Militia. 22 Feb - 27 Apr 1813. Ensign, 18 April 1814.
    Member - George Mitchell Wright [221/506]

A CHRONICLE OF SOLDIERS, SEAMEN, AND MARINES

WRIGHT, John
  b. 20 Aug 1789, Baltimore, MD
  d. Jan 1875
  m. Rebecca Leaf
  Service: 2nd Corporal, Franklin Artillery, Maryland Militia.
  Member - Alfred J. Carr [20/181]
      James Edward Carr, Jr. [10/174]
      William Edwin Carr [119/508]
      Ernest Howard [22/183]
      John Randolph Wright [3/168]

WRIGHT, William Alfred
  b. 4 Feb 1793, Essex Co., VA
  d. 7 May 1858, Essex Co., VA
  Service: Captain, War of 1812.
  Member - Thomas Wright Meade [417/2228]

YOUNG, Jacob
  b. 1795
  d. 1875, Hanover, PA
  m. Maria Eichelberger
  Service: Private, Captain Metscor's Company, Pennsylvania Mitilia. Attached to Maryland Militia. 24 Aug - 12 Sep 1814.
  Member - George Young Klinefelter [466/2558]

YOUNKER, Francis
  b.
  d. 1849, Baltimore, MD
  Service: Private, American Artillerists, Maryland Militia.
  Member - John Stuart MacDonald [188/966]

ZACHARIAS, Daniel
  b. 6 Apr 1777, Frederick Co., MD
  d. 24 Apr 1815, Frederick Co., MD
  m. Susannah Sherman, 16 Jan 1810
  Service: Captain of a troop of Cavalry bearing his name, 2nd Rgt., Maryland Militia. 7 Aug - 10 Sep 1814.
  Member - John Milton Reifsnider [241/1147]

A CHRONICLE OF SOLDIERS, SEAMEN, AND MARINES

ZIMMERMAN, David
    b. 1786, Westmoreland Co., PA
    d. 10 Mar 1857, Westmoreland Co., PA
    m. Mary Kelly, 11 May 1815, Hatlenton, PA
    Service: Private, Captain Donaldson's Company, Snider's Rgt., Pennsylvania Militia.
        25 Sep - Nov 1812.
    Member - Mathias William Sample [321/1514]

ZIMMERMAN, John
    b. after 1760, Baltimore Co., MD
    d. Aug. 1836, Baltimore Co., MD
    m. Mary Hissey, 15 Jun 1798, Baltimore, MD
    Service: Private, Captain Joseph Myers Company, 1st Rgt., Maryland Militia.
        19 Aug - 30 Nov 1814.
    Member - Kenneth Edwin Zimmerman [734/4866]

ZOLLINGER, Jacob
    b. Dauphin Co., PA
    d. 5 May 1843, Harrisburg, PA
    m. Maria Stine, 17 Mar 1817, Dauphin Co., PA
    Service: Private, Captain Walker's Company, Pennsylvania Militia.
        5 Aug - 5 Dec 1814.
    Member - Andrew Reid Johnson, Jr. [457/2375]
        John Leonard Power [313/1503]

INDEX

Abbott, Charlotte - 111
Adams, *James Frederick* - 6
Adderley, Rachel - 33
Addison, *Taylor* - 7
Adreon
    -- Captain - 73
    Christian, Captain - 47
Agnew, Margaret - 89
Aisquith, -- Captain - 36, 70, 71, 81
Alexander
    -- Captain - 56
    Margaret S. - 70
    William, Captain - 69
Allen
    Elizabeth - 64
    Mary - 19
    Samuel L., Captain - 67
Alvey, Eliza Ann - 78
Amoss, -- Captain - 48
Anderson, *Richard Edward* - 89
Aperson, Eliza - 47
Ardrey, Rachel - 33
Arthurs, *Edward Ferguson* - 40
Asher, Mary - 91
Ashley, *Lawrence Irvin* - 64
Askew, Mary - 17
Athey, *Charles Burch* - 57
Atkinson, -- Captain - 42
Austin, *William Charles, Jr.* - 92
Aylette, Mary Macon - 41
Bader
    -- Captain - 109
    Dominick, Captain - 31
Bailey, Mary - 29
Bairs, -- Captain - 108
Baker
    -- - 50
    Calvin Shelton - 64
Balderston, Martha - 59
Baldwin, -- Captain - 8

Ball
    Ann Upshur - 44
    Eliza - 81
Banning, -- Captain - 87
Barder, Barbara - 99
Barnes
    Catherine - 55
    John, Captain - 56
    Sarah - 92
    William Calvin Chestnut - 26
    Wilson King - 61
    Wilson King, Jr. - 26
Barney, -- Commodore - 34, 90, 98, 107
Barton, Elizabeth Ann - 54
Baskette, *Alvin K.* - 49
Bass, Rebecca - 63
Bassett, Mary - 22
Bates, Joanna - 102
Bauer, *Richard Wingate* - 41
Baugh, Susan - 103
Baughman
    Charles Christian - 47
    Emilius Allen - 47
    Greer Harry - 47
Bausman, Eliza - 97
Bean, Jane - 41
Beatty, *John Edwin* - 26
Beaufeau, Cristine - 5
Beck, Ada - 104
Beckley, Marie Elizabeth - 105
Bedford, Anne - 9
Beers, *Walter Whitney* - 11
Bell
    -- Colonel - 105
    Jean - 71
Belt, Jane Jacob - 33
Bennett
    Edgar Harrison - 60
    Elizabeth - 42
Benson
    Carville D. - 66

INDEX

Benson
    John Oregon - 66
    Oscar Suter - 45
    Richard Stewart - 94
Berkeley, *Merrill Duane* - 86
Bernard
    Alfred Duncan - 45
    Richard Constable - 45
Berry
    John, Captain - 111
    Thomas Lansdale - 39
Bessent, *Carl Francis* - 77
Biays, Rachel - 107
Biddle, Mary - 21
Bild, Chauncey, Captain - 49
Birckhead, Christiana - 16
Bissell, *Benjamin* - 107
Black
    Eliza Jane - 73
    Elizabeth - 32
    Rebecca - 33
Blake, -- Captain - 98
Blizzard
    Arthur Keith - 14
    Dennis Craig - 14
    Dennis Frizzell - 14
    Elizabeth - 96
    William, Captain - 7, 20
Boget, Elizabeth - 6
Bond, *Arthur Cecil* - 80
Booth, Mary - 51
Bordley, *John Lawson* - 89
Bosley, -- Captain - 74
Boughton, -- - 29
Bowers, *Henry Kenneth* - 34
Bowly, Ann Lux - 102
Bowman, Susannah Wright - 86
Boyce
    Albert Page - 81
    Heyward Easter - 81
Boyd, *James Knox Polk* - 89
Boyer, -- Captain - 73

Boyle, Susanna - 77
Bradford
    Cecelia - 22
    Samuel Webster - 59
Bradley, *Melvin James* - 44
Bradshaw, -- Captain - 34
Branch
    Charles Henry Hardin - 50
    Henry - 50
Brannan, Ann Elizabeth - 53
Brannock, -- - 65
Bransby, *John C.* - 107
Brathwaite, *Peter Lloyd Woolsey* - 16
Brengle, John, Captain - 48
Brevard, Sarah - 78
Bringle, -- Captain - 63
Brinton, *Edward Harvey* - 20
Brockenborough, Elizabeth Roane - 112
Brook, -- Captain - 37
Brooke
    -- Captain - 78
    Brian Wesley - 13
    Dandridge - 13
    Dandridge William - 13
    Randall Whitney - 13
Brown
    -- Captain - 43, 72, 85
    George J., Captain - 26
    Herbert Thomas, Jr. - 23
    John, Captain - 54
    William, Captain - 29
Brunner
    Elizabeth - 91
    Margaret - 59
Bryan, *Frederic Arthur* - 9
Bryant, Martha Ann - 52
Bryd, *James Edward* - 92
Buck, -- Captain - 90
Buckingham, Nelly - 35
Bull, *Robert Berry* - 12
Bungus, Dianna - 31
Burke, -- Captain - 80

INDEX

Burneston, Elizabeth - 38
Burnett, Ann - 72
Burton, Sarah - 55
Bushey, *Arthur Clifton, Jr.* - 12
Carbery, Thomas, Captain - 7
Carey, Lee Cummins - 30
Carmichael, Ann - 52
Carr
    Alfred J. - 113
    James Edward, Jr. - 113
    William Edwin - 113
Carroll, John, Captain - 91
Carter, *Clayton Cann* - 68
Carymill, James, Captain - 79
Castle, Mary - 21
Chambers
    Lawrence Bailey - 38
    Robert Douglas - 38
Chalmer, -- Captain - 6, 60, 92
Chandler, Mary Loockerman - 101
Chapman, *Samuel Vannort* - 107
Chews, Joseph, Captain - 48
Chittenden, *Leslie William* - 67
Claggett, Eleanor Bowie - 106
Clapham, Sophia Cook - 81
Clark
    Elizabeth - 27, 85
    Mary - 9
    Raymond B., Jr. - 91
    Susannah - 109
Clarke
    John R., Captain - 43
    Mary - 69
    Susanna - 27
Clem, Elizabeth - 103
Clerke, Margaret - 41
Clopper, Elizabeth - 103
Clow, Mary - 107
Clyde, James, Captain - 69
Coat, -- Captain - 86
Coates, Margaret Allen - 30
Cobb, *John Devine, Jr.* - 63

Cochran, *Samuel Poyntz* - 10
Cock, -- Captain - 78
Cockey, Hannah (Owings) - 99
Coffee, -- Brigadier General - 49
Colbert
    Edwin Abbott - 51
    Philip Maulsby - 51
Cole
    Elizabeth - 20
    James Carroll LeGrand - 51
Coleman, *E. Richard* - 57
Collenberg, *Henry Theodore, Jr.* - 58
Collins
    Carroll Jefferson - 17
    Nelly - 62
Conrad, Elizabeth - 61
Cooke, *William Dewey* - 99, 103, 104
Cooper
    Anne - 59
    John B., Captain - 111
Corey
    George Reece - 78
    Roland Reece, Jr. - 78
Cornelius, *Thomas Reese* - 31
Corson, *Burton Francis* - 72
Corum, Jemima - 58
Cotter, -- Captain - 40
Cottman, Ann - 77
Coulter, Mariah - 81
Cox, Ann - 38
Craig, -- Captain - 36
Crever, Sarah - 69
Cromwell, Ellen - 30
Crouch, -- Captain - 96
Crouse, Eliza - 40
Cruse, Mary - 111
Cully, Sarah Ann - 42
Culver, *Francis Barnum* - 6
Cumming, -- Captain - 74
Cunningham
    Charlotte - 39
    Margaret - 38

INDEX

Curran, Ellen - 7
Cushwa, -- Captain - 103
Dabney, George, Captain - 87
Daker, Rachel - 24
Dallam, *Harry Gough* - 45
Dalton, Maria Flower - 20
Darlington, Sarah - 104
Davies, *Robert Wynter* - 67
Davis
    Diademia - 101
    Elizabeth - 55
    Matilda - 8
    Milton Wickers, Jr. - 47
    Rebecca - 92
    Susannah - 17
    Violet - 22
    William Custis Carroll - 110
Dawes, Caroline - 75
Deal, *John Thomas, Jr.* - 98
Dean
    Martha - 89
    Rebecca - 17
Deardoff, Elizabeth - 93
Decker, -- Captain - 6
Deems, -- Captain - 42, 58, 75
Dell
    Albert Hampson - 76
    Charles Squires - 76
    Samuel Mills - 76
    Thomas Medairy - 76
    Thomas Medairy, Jr. - 76
Dennis, *James Teackle* - 111
Denny, Rachel - 6
Deputy, Comfort - 109
Dickerson, Catherine - 75
Dickey
    Charles Herman - 90
    Edmund Sadtler - 90
    Francis George - 90
    Philip Sadtler - 90
Diggs, *Ross Miles* - 34
Dobbin, Margaret - 65

Dobbins, Archibald, Captain - 68
Dolliver, *Alan Kemp* - 59
Donaldson, -- Captain - 114
Doogan, Eliza - 108
Dornblazer, John, Captain - 74
Dorney, *Charles Polk* - 35
Dorsey
    -- Captain - 100
    Eliza Ann - 41
    Elizabeth Worthington - 8
    Mary Elizabeth - 40
    Thomas Lee - 53
    Vachel Paul - 53
Douglass
    Benjamin Dun - 35
    Eliza - 33
    Robert Dun - 35
    Robert Graham Dun - 35
    Rudolph A.A. - 108
Downie, George, Commodore - 68
Downing, Sally - 95
Downs, *Samuel Addison* - 78
Dukes, *Alexander Thompson* - 78
Dunn, Ellen - 86
DuPont, -- Captain - 42
Durbin, -- Captain - 74
Durham, -- - 64
Duvall
    Martha - 12
    Richard Mareen - 37, 105
Dykins, Phoebe - 79
Earbaugh, John - 7
Earnshaw, Daniel J. - 32
Easter
    Arthur Miller - 61
    James Miller - 61
Eastwood, *Ralph Allen, Sr.* - 80
Eccleston, -- Captain - 110
Edelen, *Corlian William* - 96
Edmondson
    Ann Jane - 97
    Elizabeth - 104

INDEX

Edmonston, Edward, Captain - 31
Edwards, Mary Elizabeth - 57
Eichelberger, Maria - 113
Ellender, Catharine - 78
Elliott, *Thomas Ireland* - 21
Ellyson, Sarah - 50
Elting, -- Captain - 95
Ely, Pleasance - 35
England, *Charles* - 75
Englar, *David F.* - 74
Ennis, -- Captain - 109
Ent, George W., Captain - 92
Erhardt
    Clement Dumont, Jr. - 85
    Clement Dumont, III - 85
Evans
    -- Captain - 30, 88
    Clarence Richard - 28
Everngam
    Douglas Howard - 11
    George Gregg - 11
Fainoll, Sarah A. - 100
Farmer, Nathan, Captain - 77
Faulkner, *Nelson Franklin, Jr.* - 83
Felty, Anna Eva - 96
Fenstermacher, Barbara - 60
Fenwick, Susan - 31
Fester, Sarah - 79
Fields, Margaret - 36
Finch
    Ronald Milton - 14
    Willard Robert - 14
Finley, *Luke William* - 22
Fisher, Benjamin, Captain - 105
Fitch, Elizabeth - 103
Fleming, Allison Sweeney - 71
Fletcher, Mary - 54
Focke
    Ferdinand B. - 95
    Harry Smull - 95
    Walter David - 95
Fonsten, -- Captain - 96

Foote, Mary Stuart - 69
Ford
    Henry Jones - 58
    John Drew - 87
    Mark Douglas Lederer - 87
    Thomas G. - 32
Foreman, -- Captain - 107
Forrest, Ann - 93
Foster
    Amelia Jane - 26
    Clarence Dulany - 36
    Dulany - 36
    James, Captain - 6, 55, 102
    Lucy - 112
    Sarah - 79
Foustiens, -- Captain - 21
Fowler
    Henry, Captain - 111
    Samuel Robert, Jr. - 63
Frank, Catherine - 51
Frazier, Mary E. - 98
Freeburger, *Alexander Cooper* - 29
Freeland, *Samuel Lyles* - 27
Freeman, Rebecca - 106
French, Catherine - 6
Friend, -- Captain - 102
Frizzell
    -- Captain - 72
    William, Captain - 45
Gamerothe, Mary Magdalene - 43
Gardiner, -- Lieutenant - 17
Gardner, Mary - 45
Garland, Ann - 53
Garmin, Sarah - 110
Garner, Ann - 95
Garry, -- Captain - 19
Gartman, Mary Magdalena - 61
Gaus, Arthur D. - 75
Gegan, Elisa - 108
George
    Polly - 43
    Thomas Stevens - 17

INDEX

George
    Thomas Stevens, Jr. - 17
Getzendanner, -- Captain - 59, 91, 96
Geyert, Elizabeth - 67
Gibson, Elizabeth - 39
Gieske
    Edward Trenholm, Jr. - 107
    James Chapman - 107
Gill, Stephen, Captain - 22
Glenn, Eliza Anderson - 54
Glotfelty, Eva Margaret - 37
Goddard
    Ann - 84
    Calvin Hooker - 5
Gold, *William Buchanan, Jr.* - 95
Goldsmith, Mary Ann - 59
Gonzales, Josephine - 57
Gorrich, Sarah - 107
Gorsuch
    -- Captain - 58
    Harriett - 36, 82
Gott, Anna Maria - 74
Gould
    Barbara - 82
    Lytelton Bowen - 12
Grant, Marcia - 55
Green
    Alfred Laland - 43
    Edwin Bernard - 28
    Edwin Bernard, Jr. - 28
    Gregory Howison - 53
    May - 102
    Richard Ellwood - 28
    Samuel Alexander, Jr. - 53
    Samuel Edward, 3rd - 32
    Thomas Neven - 78
Greer, Susan - 15
Gregory, -- Captain - 75
Griffin
    Mary - 48
    Sarah - 27
Grindall, *Charles Sylvester* - 7

Guiton, -- Captain - 46
Guy, *William Burton, Jr.* - 46
Hackett, Henrietta Jane - 10
Hadel, *Albert Kimberly* - 61
Hagerman, Eliza - 65
Hagerty, Elizabeth - 97
Haines, Johana - 15
Hair, Martha - 82
Hall
    Elizabeth Bowie - 110
    Mary - 47
    Summerfield Davis - 82
Haller, Susanna Margaretha - 40
Hambleton, *Richard Nicolai* - 103
Hammond, -- Captain - 90
Hamphill, -- Captain - 104
Hancock, *James Etchberger* - 33, 39
Handy, *John Custis* - 70
Hanna, -- Captain - 55
Hardenbergh, -- Lieutenant Colonel - 39
Hargett, *Douglass H.* - 21
Harnett, *Maurice A., III* - 77
Harris
    -- Captain - 70
    Elizabeth Dodswell - 15
    Jane Campbell - 112
    Joseph Norris - 43
    Mary Ann - 66
    William Barney - 9
    William Barney, Jr. - 9
Harrison, -- General - 108
Haubert, -- Captain - 12, 51, 58, 62
Hawkins, Mary - 57, 94
Healy, Sarah - 98
Heath, -- Captain - 61, 83
Hellfenstein, Charity - 75
Hendrick, *John Burford, Jr.* - 25
Henning, Sarah - 11
Henry, -- Captain - 32
Herbert, Jane - 20
Herman, *William Focke* - 95
Hickman, Caroline - 8

INDEX

Hill
    Benjamin Dunlap, Jr. - 43
    John Philip - 25
Hisky
    John Guido - 93
    Thomas Foley - 93
    William George - 93
Hissey, Mary - 114
Hitchcock, Elenore C. - 106
Hiteshew, Martha - 74
Hock, Elizabeth - 25
Holden, *Irvin* - 82
Holland, Elizabeth - 70
Hollinger, *Edwin Theodore* - 34
Holloway
    Charles Thomas, II - 88
    Reuben Ross - 88
Hollyday, *Thomas Worthington* - 112
Hood, -- Colonel - 105
Hook, -- Captain - 86
Hoomes, Armestead, Captain - 41
Hooper
    Mary - 76, 82
    Sara - 39
    Stuart Cator - 18
Hopkins
    Carroll Creswell - 57
    Henry Powell - 24
    Henry Powell, Jr. - 24
    Joseph Carroll - 57
    Sarah - 19
Houck, William - 51
Hough
    John Edward - 100
    Pliny Miles - 100
Houghton, *Ira Holden* - 72
Howard
    Benjamin, Captain - 85
    Elizabeth Rowe - 74
    Stanley Lewis - 72
Howerton, -- Captain - 54
Howlett, Mary Ann - 68

Huddleson, *James Howard, Jr.* - 99
Hughes, Louisa - 7
Hunt, -- Captain - 86
Hutchins, Elizabeth Ann - 109
Hutchison, *William Brown* - 89
Hyde, *Edward Duncan* - 81
Hye, Sarah - 83
Iglehart, *James Davidson* - 32
Inloes, *Joseph Howard* - 88
Irons, Ann Catherine - 18
Isaac, Hannah - 37
Isaacs, -- Captain - 105
Jacks, -- Captain - 6
Jackson
    -- - 22
    Sarah D. - 12
    Thomas, Captain - 37
Jacob
    Jemina - 47
    Rachel - 66
Jacobs
    Jemima - 87
    Rachel - 66
Jarvis, Ann - 31
Jenkins, -- Captain - 71
Jenness, *Herbert Leon* - 102
John, -- Captain - 23
Johnson
    Andrew Reid, Jr. - 114
    Sarah - 43
Jones
    -- Captain - 17
    Charlotte - 10
    Edward Graham, Jr. - 94
    Edward Graham, III - 94
    Emily Pemberton - 50
    Harriet - 85
    John R., Captain - 85
    Mary - 86
Juett, William, Captain - 100
Kane, -- Captain - 16

INDEX

Keen
    George Benson - 94
    Mary - 71
Keets, Margaret - 14
Keith
    -- Captain - 41
    Chloe - 41
Kelly
    -- Captain - 30
    Mary - 114
Kemp
    Charles Edward - 15, 48, 84, 92, 96
    Joseph, Captain - 88
Kenly, *William Watkins* - 106
Kennedy, -- Captain - 68
Kerlenger, John, Captain - 40
Ketterman, M. Louisa - 62
Kidd, Rebecca Ann - 57
Kielman
    L.E. - 87
    Toxie L. - 87
Kierstead, -- Captain - 60
Kinney, Matilda - 99
Kirlinger, J., Captain - 42
Klinefelter, *George Young* - 113
King
    Charles Alfred Ely - 39
    Margareth Elizabeth - 86
Kloman, *Antony Joseph Trapnell* - 5
Knadler, *Robert Warren* - 37
Knight, Samuel B., Captain - 43
Koenig, John Lance - 72
Koontz
    Amos R. - 46
    James W. - 46
Kratz, *Charles Irving, Jr.* - 88
Krebs, Mary - 89
Kreidler, Elizabeth - 79
Lambdin, Sara - 91
Lambert, Martha - 11
Lamping, *William* - 97
Lanahan, *William Wallace* - 85

Lantz, Maria - 48
Latane, Elizabeth - 105
Lawrason, Alice - 87
Leaf, Rebecca - 113
Leahy, Mary - 9
Leber, *Henry Hoke* - 42
Lee
    -- Captain - 45
    Cassandra - 46
    Howard Hall Macy - 41
Leeke, Mary - 32
Lehmann
    Brent Dawson - 38
    Leslie Sexton - 38
    Wallace Kemp - 38, 59
Lemon, Nancy - 111
Lescure, *William Joseph, 3rd* - 68
Levering, -- Captain - 108
Levly, Elizabeth - 49
Linthicum, Abner, Captain - 94
Lloyd
    Mary Tayloe - 61
    William Henry - 16
Long
    Elizabeth - 48
    Margaret - 7
    Mariah - 66
Loose, *John Ward Willson* - 69
Loux, Barbara - 95
Lowry
    Elizabeth - 90
    Nathan Parks - 37
    Robert Kelly - 37
Lowrye, -- Captain - 71
Luce, Elizabeth - 95
Luckett, *Robert Leven* - 29
Lusby, Susan - 18
Lyons, *Robert Ellsworth* - 106
Macatee, -- Captain - 22
MacCarthy, *Howard, Jr.* - 50
Maccubbin, Mary Ann - 60
MacDonald, *John Stuart* - 113

INDEX

Mackenheimer, Margaret - 36
Mackenzie, *George Norbury* - 36
Mackey
    -- Captain - 40
    Harold Kenneth - 70
MacKubin, Mary Ann - 60
Magee, -- Captain - 54
Magheris, Peter, Captain - 32
Maglidt, *Henry Wilson* - 111
Magruder, -- Captain - 97, 103
Mahool, *John Barry* - 13
Maloney, *James Aloysius* - 46
Maltbie, *William Henry* - 104
Manning, *Richard Charles, III* - 95
Marbury, *Francis Cross* - 93
Marine
    Madison - 62
    Richard Elliott - 62
    William Matthew - 62
Marr
    Margaret - 88
    Robert E.L. - 73
    William G. - 73
Marsten, -- Captain - 101
Marston, *James Graham* - 24
Martens, J.B., Captain - 26
Martin
    Harry Culver - 77
    Joseph Pentz - 82
    Sarah - 67
Massey
    Frances H. - 91
    Joshua W., Captain - 91
Massie, *Cecil Miles, Sr.* - 83
Maxwell, Anne - 23
Maynadier, *Thomas Murray* - 16
McArthur, -- Captain - 112
McBlair, Alice - 88
McCabes, -- Captain - 50
McCarty, Margaret - 34
McCenie, Sallie - 80
McClough, Mary - 107

McColgan, *Edward* -85
McConkey, -- Captain - 21
McConnel, -- - 99
McCoy, Charlotte - 26
McCullough, Mary - 77
McCurley
    Felix - 46
    James Wallace - 42, 45, 46
McDonald, *William Bartholow* - 82
McDonnell, *Austin McCarthy* - 69
McElderry
    -- Captain - 14
    Mary - 35
McEvers, Catherine Augustas - 13
McFadden
    A. Weems - 18
    Archibald George William - 19
McGaw, Elizabeth - 46
McGlathery, Rebecca - 97
McKinnell, *William Wendell Bollman* - 16
McKown, *Barrett Lee* - 83
McMechen, Tabitha - 78
McMullin, -- Captain - 94
McMullins, Margareth - 13
McRae, -- Captain - 25
Meade, *Thomas Wright* - 113
Mears
    Adelbert Warren - 12
    Christian Emmerich - 12, 80
Meriken, Sarah - 108
Meriweather, Louisa - 66
Merrill, *George Grenville* - 65
Merritt, *James Miller* - 68
Metscor, -- Captain - 113
Metzger
    Elizabeth - 58
    Fred, Captain - 96
Meyers, Catherine - 93
Michel, *Robert Emory* - 111
Middendorf, *John William, Jr.* - 99
Middleton, *Arthur Pierce* - 31
Milber, -- Captain - 64

INDEX

Miller
    John Henry - 95
    Maria Eve - 63
Mincher, Ann - 58
Mines, Elizabeth - 62
Minetree, Virginia - 25
Mitchell, *Frank Paull, Jr.* - 101
Moale, -- Captain - 56, 66
Mohler, *Isaac Wimbert, Jr.* - 5
Money, Ruth - 43
Montague, William L., Captain - 112
Montgomery
    -- Captain - 96
    Anne - 26
    John, Captain - 76
    Sarah - 50
Moore
    -- Captain - 77
    Beverly Polk - 94
    Christopher Polk - 94
    Eugene Nelson - 36
    Sarah Lyttleton - 5
Morgan
    John Hurst - 12
    Philip Sidney - 12
Morling, *Frank L.* - 107
Morris
    George, Captain - 83
    John Delashmutt - 35
Moses, -- Captain - 79
Moylan, *Charles Ellsworth, Jr.* - 45
Munnikhuysen, *John Bryarly* - 46
Murphy, Mary Ann - 36, 46
Murray
    -- Captain - 72
    Rachel Rebecca - 97
    Sally Scott - 67
Myers
    Henry, Captain - 24
    Joseph, Captain - 114
    Joseph A. - 44
    Philip - 74

Myers
    Philip, III - 74
Nace, -- - 72
Nash, *Charles W.* - 33
Naylor, Hannah - 47
Neagle, Sarah T. - 22
Nelson
    Lucy T. - 83
    Nancy - 100
Newcomb, *Fred Norman* - 21
Newell, John Davis - 100
Nicholson, -- Captain - 38, 40
Norris
    Abell Archibald, Jr. - 10
    Juliet - 56
    Nancy - 96
Odenbaugh, Mary - 54
Offutt, *Thomas Worthington* - 56
Orem, *John Henry, Jr.* - 91
Orme, Anne V. - 64
Osborn, Phoebe - 44
Osburn, Nicholas, Captain - 29
Overington
    John - 11
    Robert Bruce - 11
Owens
    Ameilia - 19
    Edward Burneston - 20
    Edward Burneston, Jr. - 20, 23
    Franklin Buchanan - 67
Owings, -- Captain - 87
Page, *Henry Littleton, III* - 33
Pardee, *Ernest Lewis* - 38
Parnham, -- Captain - 70
Parr
    Guy Hudson, Jr. - 15, 89
    Lee Sutherland - 15
Parrish, *William Fleming* - 112
Patterson, Mary - 40
Paul, Martha - 35
Peden, *Henry Clint, Jr.* - 8
Penn, John - 89

INDEX

Pennington, -- Captain - 61, 101
Peregoy, *Frederick Charles* - 20
Peter, Michael, Captain - 21
Peters
    -- Captain - 110
    -- Major - 60
    Winfield - 43
Peterson, Mary - 100
Petre, Michael - Captain - 95
Pettis, -- Captain - 68
Phifer, *Robert Smith, Jr.* - 54
Pierpoint, Mary - 71
Pierson, -- Captain - 29
Pike, Nancy - 24
Pinney, Peter, Captain - 62
Piper, -- Captain - 28, 57, 82
Pitcher
    Griffith Fontaine - 48, 83
    William Henry, Jr. - 42, 83
Plowdon, Mary Ann - 56
Polk, Whittington, Captain - 75
Poole, Anne - 47
Popham, Grace - 101
Porter
    -- Captain - 19
    Robert Lee, Jr. - 20
Power, *John Leonard* - 114
Primrose, *Samuel Fletcher* - 54
Pritchard, *Arthur John* - 98
Pryor
    William Brand - 8
    William Young - 8
Pugh
    William Nussear Stevenson - 53
    William Nussear Stevenson, Jr. - 53
Pumphrey, Charles, Captain - 111
Quinn, Sarah - 72
Raab, Ann Barbara - 16
Rahute, Sarah Williams - 102
Railley, Elizabeth - 29
Raitt, Barbara Arianna - 49
Ramsay, Elizabeth Johnson - 14

Randall, *Watson Beale* - 101, 106
Rasmussen, *Tom Niel* - 103
Raven, Isaac, Captain - 53
Rea, -- Captain - 72
Reagan, Margaret - 88
Reed, Robert, Captain - 100
Reese
    Catharine - 69
    Catherine - 20
    Howard Hopkins - 23
    Maria Keener - 60
Regester, *Robert Thomas* - 102
Reid, Ameilia - 32
Reifsnider, *John Milton* - 113
Remsberg, Elizabeth - 92
Reynolds, Sarah - 75
Richardson
    Audbrey DeVaughn - 112
    Horace Kimball - 13
Rider, -- Captain - 62
Riggin, Priscilla - 83
Riggs, *Robert Meldrum* - 41
Rinehart
    Evan Warden - 88
    Thomas Warden, 88
Ringgold, -- Captain - 37
Rinker, Abraham, Captain - 60
Rittenhouse, *Samuel Albert* - 21
Roberts
    Martha - 87
    Robert Leonard - 104
    Robert Leonard, Jr. - 104
Robertson, *George Sadtler* - 90
Robinson, Martha - 84
Rochelle, Mary Hart - 64
Roger, -- Captain - 5, 19
Rogers, -- Captain - 107
Rolle, Elizabeth H. - 88
Roney, -- Captain - 19
Roosa, Rachel - 39
Rose, Caroline - 52
Ross, Maria - 34

INDEX

Rossmann, *Edward Albert* - 93
Rothrock, -- Captain - 87
Rumbley, Elizabeth - 17
Russell, Rachel - 73
Rutter
    Ann - 80
    Anne - 21
Saborn, Deborah - 13
Sadtler
    Lucien MacDowell - 42
    Philip B., Captain - 86
Saffron, Sarah Ann - 5
Sale, Cornelius, Captain - 89
Sample, Mathias William - 114
Samuels, Margaret - 79
Sand, -- Captain - 93
Sanders, *George Francis* - 87
Sands, Mary Jane - 76
Sanford
    John Lowry - 105
    William Lanahan - 105
Sangston, *Laurence Purdy* - 5
Sauerwein, Catherine Captio - 90
Saunders, *Willard Gerald, II* - 66
Scarborough, -- Captain - 12
Schaeffer, Margarette, 108
Schiaffino
    Ashton - 6
    George Evans - 6
Schlenker, *Richard Carl* - 74
Schoffield, Anne - 19
Schrim, -- Captain - 92
Schwarzaner, -- Captain - 11
Schwarzouer, -- Captain - 84
Scott
    Elizabeth - 78
    Frank Bertram - 53
Selby, Elizabeth - 93
Sellers, Elizabeth - 6
Sewell
    Mary - 55
    Sarah - 24

Seymour, Fanny - 89
Sharp
    Alfred Elliott - 15
    Alfred Elliott, Jr. - 15
Shaw, Jerusha Anne - 105
Shehan
    Daniel Edward - 31
    J. Brooke - 31
    Robert James - 31
    William Henry - 31
    William Henry, Jr. - 31
Sheib, Samuel Henry - 38
Shepley, Mary - 104
Sherman, Susannah - 113
Sherwood, -- Captain - 11
Shield, Elizabeth - 6
Shields, Mary - 94
Shipley, Rachel Owings - 112
Shoemaker, *Michael Meyers* - 97
Showers, -- Captain - 106
Shriner
    Edward Derr, Jr. - 91
    Mary - 96
Shriver
    Alfred Jenkins - 56
    Catherine - 109
Shryer, Sarah - 88
Shuck, Mary - 15
Shumate, Celia - 54
Sillman, Sarah - 72
Simmons, -- Captain - 80
Simpson
    -- Captain - 24
    Harriet Worthington - 48
Sioussat, *St. George Charles Leakin* - 65
Sism, Jane - 32
Skinner, *Maurice Edward* - 58
Slacum
    Margaret - 63
    Mary Boyne - 63
Slicer, -- Captain - 25, 94
Sloan, *Ralph Wiley* - 109

INDEX

Slorripe, Sarah - 24
Slothower, *Henry* - 25
Small, -- - 27
Smalling, Mary - 75
Smallwood, Cassandra - 27
Smith
    -- Captain - 50
    Andrew, Captain - 71
    Elizabeth - 11
    Francis Scott Key - 61
    George Long - 50
    Nancy - 72
    Sarah - 110
    Winfield Ross - 18
Smithson
    -- Captain - 48
    John, Captain - 34, 109
Snider, *Ernest L.* - 37, 79
Snook, Lydia A. - 84
Snow, *Henry* - 55
Snowden, -- Captain - 111
Snyder, Julianna - 34
Sommerville, Mary - 21
Sothoron, -- Captain - 50
Southerland, *Edwin Williams* - 63
Sower, -- Captain - 103
Spalding, Ann - 56
Spangler, -- Captain - 79
Sparks, Rachel - 100
Spencer
    Ann - 39
    Susanna - 50
Spicer, -- Captain - 57
Spragins
    Samuel Hamilton, Jr. - 47
    Samuel Hamilton, III - 47
St. Clair, Martha - 99
Stansbury, -- Captain - 20, 102
Steele, Frances Allanly - 100
Steever, -- Captain - 16, 45
Stein, *Charles Francis, Jr.* - 48
Steiner, -- Captain - 97

Stelle, Elizabeth Hooten - 72
Stephens, Sylvia - 13
Sterett, -- Captain - 80, 84
Sterling, *Thomas King Nelson* - 100
Sterret, -- Captain - 18
Sterrett, -- Captain - 103
Steuart, -- Captain - 106
Stevens, -- Lieutenant - 13
Stevenson, Elizabeth - 101
Stewart
    -- Captain - 52
    Ambler Jones - 10
    Carl Hoak, Jr. - 88
    Donald Franklin - 34
Stick
    Gordon Malvern Fair, Jr. - 40, 92
    Gordon Malvern Fair, Sr. - 40
    Thomas Howard Fitchett - 40, 105
Stickney, Charlotte - 85
Stiles, -- Captain - 33, 43, 109
Stillwell, Ann - 99
Stine, Maria - 114
Stitt, Nancy - 73
Stockdale, -- Captain - 53
Stockwell, Phebe - 73
Stocton, -- Captain - 66
Stoehr, Daniel - 96
Stonestreet, -- Captain - 72
Street, *Edward Parker* - 16
Stricker, -- - 83
Strickland, David, Captain - 89
Stull
    Ann Elizabeth - 96
    John J., Captain - 31
Stunp, Frederick, Captain - 103
Summers, *Walter Penrose* - 46
Sutton, *Fredus Edmund* - 81
Sweney, Elizabeth Sprigg - 62
Swift, Charlotte - 15
Talbott, *Hattersly Worthington, Jr.* - 110
Tarr, *Frederick Crey* - 30

INDEX

Taylor
    Edmund, Captain - 86
    Ruth - 14
Thomas
    -- Captain - 104
    Benjamin, Captain - 109
    Eliza Snowden - 65
    Maria - 53
    Polly - 30
    Sarah Ellis - 28
    Turbey F., Lieutenant - 106
Thompson
    -- Captain - 57, 93
    Ann - 94
    Raymond Webb - 102
Thomsen, *Roszel Cathcart* - 23
Thorp, Elizabeth - 110
Tilghman
    -- Colonel - 110
    Anna Maria - 18
Tinges, *Charles Howard* - 107
Travers, John, Captain - 82
Trueheart, *Herbert Lee* - 20
Tschudi
    Harold - 103
    Samuel Werner - 103
Tschudy, Ann - 91
Tucker
    -- Captain - 52
    Brinson Cumming - 30
    James Armstrong Owings - 52
Tull, *Willis Clayton, Jr.* - 75
Turbett, -- Captain - 8
Turnbull
    -- Captain - 15
    Nicholas, Captain - 84
Turner
    -- Captain - 10
    Elizabeth - 105
    John, Captain - 34, 109
    Mary - 7
Tuthill, Freegift, Captain - 79

Utz, Magdalene - 14
Van Heckel, Elizabeth - 81
Van Horn, *Arthur* - 95
Vaughan, *Edwin Steuart* - 97
Vaughn, Alomira K. - 83
Veazy, Rebecca - 26
Vinson
    -- Captain - 10
    Parthena - 70
von der Hoof, Ann Maria - 90
Wade, *Samuel Henry* - 90
Waggaman, Elizabeth - 61
Waite, Matilda - 23
Walker
    -- Captain - 114
    William Samuel Crittenden - 30
Wall, *Alfred Vernon* - 25
Waller, Philis Lowe - 44
Waltham, Eliza - 37
Ward
    Elizabeth Stickney - 49
    Nicholas Donnell - 33
    William Ray - 34
Warfield
    -- Captain - 16, 25
    Ann Maria - 80
    Edwin - 106
    Sarah - 10
Waring
    Benjamin Harrison - 11
    William Emory, Jr. - 65
Warner
    -- Captain - 65
    Anne Olney - 35
    Dorothea A. - 76
    Elizabeth - 94
Waters, *S.K. Fendall* - 99
Watkins, Selina Ann - 67
Watson, *David Coleman* - 27
Watts, -- Captain - 21
Webb, *Edmund Joseph, Jr.* - 59
Webster, Amelia - 92

INDEX

Weisheit, *Joseph Elmer, Sr.* - 80
Weller, Elizabeth - 52
Wells
    Charles Joseph - 27
    Lydia - 98
    William John, Jr. - 22
Wemple, Rebecca - 29
Wetter, *John King* - 81
Wheatly, Mary M. - 70
Wheeler
    Ellen - 48
    Frances Helen - 56
    Sarah - 45
White
    Ann G. - 77
    Clarissa - 6
    Fannie - 46
    William, Captain - 87
    William Zebulon - 106
Whiteford
    Daniel Francis Xavier - 110
    Lingard Ignatius - 110
    Lingard Ignatius, Jr. - 110
Whitesides, Sarah - 103
Whitney, Elizabeth - 11
Whyte, *William Pinkney, Jr.* - 83
Wight, *Oliver Birckhead* - 38
Wilcox, Eleanor - 57
Wilhelm, Christina - 42
Williams
    Charles Herman - 51
    Frances - 28
    Mark Mansfield - 51
Williamson
    Fletcher Phillips - 82
    Jeffrey Phillips - 82
    Thomas Wilson - 46
Wilmoth, *Harold Edgar* - 55
Wilson
    -- Captain - 26, 74
    Gerrard, Captain - 27
    Samuel, Captain - 34

Winder, William H. Colonel - 60, 77
Winslow
    Caleb, Jr. - 65
    Caleb, Sr. - 65
    John Leiper, Jr. - 65
    Nathan John - 65
Wirt, Laura - 84
Wisler, Anna Nancy - 69
Wolf, Mary - 53
Wonderly, Maria Barbara - 51
Wood
    Bathsheba - 7
    Robert Spencer - 79
Wooden, *Ernest Elmer* - 55
Woods
    -- Captain - 73
    William, Captain - 26
Woodward
    Henry, Captain - 92
    Jane Maria - 9
Woolford, Roger, Captain - 65
Worthington
    Miltenberger Hall, Jr. - 76
    Thomas Carroll, Jr. - 60
Young
    Gary Edward - 70
    Howard Edward - 108
Ziegler, Barbara - 40
Zimmerman
    Catherine - 18
    Raymond Nathan, Jr. - 60

ADDENDA

LEPPO, Jacob
    b. 27 Dec 1789, Carroll Co., MD
    d. after 1862, Carroll Co., MD
    m. Susanna Miller, 10 Feb 1818, Baltimore Co., MD
    Service: Private, Captain William Blizzard's Company, Colonel Nace's Rgt.
        19 Aug - 10 Sep 1813.
    Member - George Duane Leatherwood Berry [746/4968]

LONG, Christian
    b. 1791, MD or PA
    d. Mar 1861, Carroll Co., MD
    m. Elen --, circa 1822, MD or PA
    Service: Private, Captain William Murray's Company, 36th Rgt.
        25 Aug - 27 Oct 1814.
    Member - Francis Brent Seville [747/4969]

APPENDIX

OFFICERS

of the

SOCIETY OF THE WAR OF 1812

in the

STATE OF MARYLAND

MILITARY COMMANDERS

First Military Commander

Major General Samuel Smith

(1814 to 1815)

Second Military Commander

Major General George H. Steuart

(1815 to 1841)

PRESIDENTS

* Maj. Gen. William McDonald	Veteran of 1812	1841-1845
* Col. David Harris	Veteran of 1812	1845-1847
* Major William Jackson	Veteran of 1812	1847-1848
* Col. Joseph K. Stapleton	Veteran of 1812	1848-1852
* Capt. Andrew E. Warner, Sr	Veteran of 1812	1852-1871
* Maj. Joshua Dryden	Veteran of 1812	1871-1879
* Capt. John J. Daneker	Veteran of 1812	1879-1882
* Col. Elijah Stansbury	Veteran of 1812	1882-1884
* James C. Morford	Veteran of 1812	1884-1889

† Samuel A. Downs	1889 to 1890
† James Hyland	1890 to 1891
† Louis P. Griffith	1891 to 1894
Hon. Edwin Warfield	1894 to 1898
James Edward Carr, Jr.	1898 to 1901
John Mason Dulany	1901 to 1903
Albert Kimberly Hadel, M.D.	1903 to 1905
Brig. Gen. Peter Leary, U.S.A.	1905 to 1911
James D. Iglehart	1911 to 1914
Alfred D. Bernard	1914 to 1916
Charles E. Sadtler, M.D.	1916 to 1917
Alfred J. Carr (died in office)	1917 to Jan. 29, 1923
Thomas M. Maynadier	1923 to 1926
Maj. Gen. Clinton Levering Riggs	1926 to 1929
James Etchberger Hancock	1929 to 1941
John Henry Orem, Jr (died in office)	1941 to Feb. 16, 1942
John L. Sanford	1942 to 1943
James Etchberger Hancock	1943 to 1945
Lt. Col. George E. Ijams, ARNG	1945 to 1946
Hon. George Washington Williams	1946 to 1948
William Henry Pitcher	1948 to 1950
John A. Pentz	1950 to 1953
S. Denmead Kolb	1953 to 1956
Charles Francis Stein	1956 to 1958
C. Elliott Baldwin	1958 to 1962
Herbert Lee Trueheart	1962 to 1964
Robert Emory Michel	1964 to 1966
Gordon Malvern Fair Stick	1966 to 1968
William Henry Lloyd (died in office)	1968 to Sep. 21, 1969
Lt. Col. Curtis Carroll Davis, USAR (Ret.)	1969 to 1972
Dennis Frizzell Blizzard	1972 to 1974
Hon. Wilson King Barnes	1974 to 1976
Edward Charles Beetem, II	1976 to 1978
S. Vannort Chapman	1978 to 1980
Clement D. Erhardt, Jr.	1980 to 1982
Richard Nicolai Hambleton	1982 to 1984
Gordon Malvern Fair Stick, Jr.	1984 to 1986
Col. Samuel A. Rittenhouse, USAR (Ret.)	1986 to 1988
Wilson King Barnes, Jr.	1988 to 1990
Carl F. Bessent	1990 to 1992
Brig. Gen. Edward Graham Jones, Jr., ARNG (Ret.)	1992 to

* Association of Defenders
† Association of Descendants

SECRETARIES

Capt. Samuel Myers	Veteran	1841 to 1845
Howard Griffith	Veteran	1845 to 1846
Edward Roberts	Veteran	1846 to 1848
Howard Griffith	Veteran	1848 to 1851
Col. Nicholas Brewer	Veteran	1851 to 1880
William H. Daneker		1881 to 1889
Lewis H. Miller		1889 to 1891
Albert Kimberly Hadel, M.D.		1891 to 1892
John Edwin Warner		1892 to 1893
Arthur M. Easter		1893 to 1894
William Harrison Gill		1894 to 1895
James Davidson Iglehart, M.D.		1895 to 1901
Charles Edward Teale		1901 to 1909
Thomas Wilson Williamson		1909 to 1910
Ross Miles Diggs		1910 to 1911
John Custis Handy		1911 to 1917
Charles F. Henderson		1917 to 1919
John Custis Handy		1919 to 1920
James Davidson Iglehart, M.D.		1920 to 1923
Richard Constable Bernard		1923 to 1932
William Henry Pitcher, Jr.		1932 to 1938
Philip Myers		1938 to 1942
John A. Pentz		1942 to 1947
Henry T. Collenberg, Jr.		1947 to 1949
Thomas Wright Meade		1949 to 1950
David F. Englar, Jr.		1950 to 1951
Joseph Elliott Green, Jr.		1951 to 1956
John Thomas Shehan		1956 to 1957
Leslie William Chittenden		1957 to 1958
E. Richard Coleman		1958 to 1963

CORRESPONDING SECRETARIES

E. Richard Coleman	1963 to 1984
Edward Graham Jones, Jr.	1984 to 1986
Stanley Lewis Howard	1986 to

RECORDING SECRETARIES

F. Bertram Scott	1963 to 1967
Bernard J. Medairy, Jr.	1967 to 1974
Walter Focke Herman	1974 to 1976
S. Vannort Chapman	1976 to 1977
Gordon Malvern Fair Stick, Jr.	1977 to 1979
James M. Merritt	1979 to 1987

Frederick N. Newcomb   1987 to

TREASURERS

Samuel Hyde	Veteran	1843 to 1846
Col. Nicholas Brewer	Veteran	1846 to 1851
Samuel Childs	Veteran	1851 to 1853
Asbury Jarrett	Veteran	1853 to 1855
Christopher Wynn	Veteran	1855 to 1861
Samuel Childs	Veteran	1861 to 1863
Asbury Jarrett	Veteran	1863 to 1865
Samuel Childs	Veteran	1865 to 1867
Asbury Jarrett	Veteran	1867 to 1882
William H. Daneker		1882 to 1883
Asbury Jarrett	Veteran	1883 to 1885
William H. Daneker		1885 to 1889
Lewis H. Miller		1889 to 1892
Robert T. Smith		1892 to 1900
James Edmondson Steuart		1900 to 1901
Edward Ferguson Arthurs		1901 to 1917
Ira Holden Houghton		1917 to 1939
Thomas Leonard Reeder		1939 to 1942
David F. Englar, Jr.		1942 to 1945
Philip Myers		1945 to 1946
William Henry Pitcher		1946 to 1949
Norris Harris		1949 to 1956
C. Elliott Baldwin		1956 to 1959
Edwin B. Green, Jr.		1959 to 1962
Dennis Frizzell Blizzard		1962 to 1965
Walter Focke Herman		1965 to 1969
Clement D. Erhardt, Jr.		1969 to 1979
Brian W. Brooke		1979 to 1982
Edwin W. Southerland		1982 to 1983
Samuel A. Rittenhouse		1983 to 1985
Willis C. Tull, Jr.		1985 to 1992
Samuel A. Rittenhouse		1992 to

MARSHALS

John Baltzel	Veteran	1842 to 1844
Seth Pollard	Veteran	1844 to 1845
Gen. Anthony Miltenberger	Veteran	1845 to 1863
John Ijams	Veteran	1863 to 1879
Col. Nicholas Brewer	Veteran	1879 to 1880
William H. Daneker		1881 to 1889
Louis H. Miller		1892 to 1893
Herbert Lee Trueheart		1955 to 1961
Carl Hoak Stewart, Jr.		1961 to 1965
George E. Linthicum, III		1965 to 1966
Henry Powell Hopkins, Jr.		1966 to 1966
Walter Focke Herman		1966 to 1967
William H. Lloyd		1967 to 1968
Donald F. Stewart		1968 to 1971
Edward C. Beetem, II		1971 to 1988
Dandridge Brooke		1988 to

REGISTRARS

Albert Kimberly Hadel, M.D.	1892 to 1903
Alfred D. Bernard	1903 to 1907
Madison Marine	1907 to 1908
Howard Hall Macey Lee	1908 to 1919
Francis Barnum Culver	1919 to 1932
Ferdinand B. Focke	1932 to 1938
Hon. George Washington Williams	1938 to 1946
Harry Roberts	1946 to 1949
John A. Pentz	1949 to 1950
Thomas Wright Meade	1950 to 1953
Joseph C. Hopkins	1953 to 1956
Dr. James Graham Marston	1956 to 1958
Harry Wright Newman	1958 to 1983
Raymond B. Clark, Jr.	1983 to 1990
Dennis Frizzell Blizzard	1990 to

GENEALOGISTS

Harry Wright Newman	1958 to 1983
Raymond B. Clark, Jr.	1983 to 1990
Henry Clint Peden, Jr.	1990 to

RECORDS AND DOCUMENTS

The Archives and Documentary Records of the Society of the War of 1812 in the State of Maryland are on file at the Langsdale Library, University of Baltimore, 1420 Maryland Avenue, Baltimore, Maryland 21201. Duplicates of application papers are on file at the Archives of the General Society of the War of 1812, located at the Lancaster County Historical Society, Lancaster, Pennsylvania.

Records are on file in the following places:

Library of Congress . . . . Washington, D.C.

Maryland State Archives . . . . Annapolis, Md.

Maryland Historical Society . . . . Baltimore, Md.

Utah Genealogical Society . . . . . . Salt Lake City, Utah

----o----

COMMEMORATIONS:

THE BATTLE OF BALTIMORE
SEPTEMBER 12-14, 1814

THE BATTLE OF NEW ORLEANS
JANUARY 8, 1815

FOUNDING OF DEFENDERS' ASSOCIATION
MAY 14, 1841

A CHRONICLE
OF WAR OF 1812 SOLDIERS,
SEAMEN, AND MARINES

added
YEAR 2000 SUPPLEMENT

YEAR 2000 SUPPLEMENT
A CHRONICLE OF WAR OF 1812 SOLDIERS, SEAMEN, AND MARINES

PREFACE

Moving beyond the century covered in the original printing of 1993, this Supplement advances the "Chronicle" into the electronic information era. The initial publication is reproduced as it was printed, with its own index and annotations. The Supplement, however, is set-up with relative indexes and notations at the conclusion of the book.

Although the chief concern for the researcher in both sections is the biographical data of the War of 1812 veterans and their descendants who took membership in the Society, the appendix of officers and archives may at times enhance the historical gleanings.

Officers of the Society whose names do not appear in the original lists are: President — Dandridge Brooke 1994-96, Lawrence B. Chambers 1996-98, M. Hall Worthington 1998-2000, George E. Linthicum 2000-; Recording Secretary — Nathan J. Winslow 1993-95, George D.L. Berry 1996-; Treasurer — M. Hall Worththington 1994-98, Barrett L. McKown 1998-; Marshal — Joseph L. Woodward 1999-.

In addition to the archive locations shown on page 138, the following electronic addresses will benefit research purposes.
General Society Website: www.societyofthewarof1812.org
Maryland Society Website: http://www.ubalt.edu/archives/swe/swe.htm

Baltimore, Maryland
July 2000

Dennis F. Blizzard
Thomas L. Hollowak

YEAR 2000 SUPPLEMENT
A CHRONICLE OF WAR OF 1812 SOLDIERS, SEAMEN, AND MARINES

NOTES

1) Membership numbers: The first number within brackets is the Maryland Society number which is followed by the General Society number.

2) When a number is followed by a "C" the member has taken the one-time allowance to use a collateral line from the veteran.

3) The suffix "S" indicates the lineage presented is supplemental to that which was first used by a member who has been elected previously.

4) Use of "D" indicates that a member holds a second or dual membership in another state, additional to but not in place of his residential state.

5) Early presidents: Some of the 19th century presidents' names may not be included in the biographical matter. Although leaders of the Association of Defenders 1841 to 1887 or of the Descendants of Defenders of Baltimore 1887 to 1893, they may have deceased before the formation of the Society of the War of 1812. The archives unfortunately have no data in regard to their vitae as members of the above organizations.

6) Corrigenda to the 1993 printing of the "Chronicle":
    p. 22   Calhoun, Adam, Jr. m. Jane Daniel
    p. 26   Coffman, Joseph, Veteran member 1893
    p. 31   Curl, Jarrott, Veteran member 1893
    p. 67   Lumberson, John, Veteran member 1893
    p. 71   McCurley, Felix b. York Co., PA
               McCurley, James Bernard, Jr.
    p. 108 Welsh, William, Veteran member 1893

YEAR 2000 SUPPLEMENT
A CHRONICLE OF WAR OF 1812 SOLDIERS, SEAMEN, AND MARINES

A CHRONICLE OF SOLDIERS, SEAMEN, AND MARINES

BELL, John
- b. 12 Jan 1779, Baltimore, MD
- d. 1860, Baltimore, MD
- m. Hannah Harlan, 5 Jan 1799, Baltimore, MD
- Service: Private in Capt. Robert Galloway's Co., 2nd Maryland Militia Reg. 27 July 1814 and 13 Oct 1814.
- Member – Clarence John Sullivan [785-C / 5449-C]

BONAWITZ, John
- b. 9 Apr 1794, Berks Co., PA
- d. 1 Mar 1888, Schuykill Co., PA
- m. Magdalena Hautz about 1813, Pine Grove, Schuykill Co., PA
- Service: Listed as Jno Bonewerts, Col. Kennedy's Rgt, 26 Aug 1814; Pvt. John Bonewitz, Inf. under Capt. John Elder, 95th Rgt., Col. Maxwell Kennedy, 5 Sep 1814.
- Member – Martin Jacob Peicker [774-D / 5019]

BUSH, Oliver
- b. 13 Aug 1770, Westfield, MA
- d. 9 Apr 1844, Turin, NY
- m. Electa Dewey, 8 Jan 1796, Westfield, MA
- Service: Major in Gen. Benedict's Rgt., NY Militia 2 Jul 1812 – 7 Jan 1813
- Member – Grahame Thomas Smallwood, Jr. [768D / 2927]

CONNOR, Levin
- b. abt. 1782, Worcester Co., MD
- d. 20 Jan 1822, Worcester Co., MD
- m. Amelia (Milly) Bowen, 2 Nov 1815, Worcester Co., MD
- Service: Lt. in Capt. Scarborough's Co. 9th Reg., 10th Brigade, Commissioned 8 Jul 1814.
- Member – James Frederick Waesche [765 / 5204]

CUMMINS, Robert
- b. abt. 1782, MD
- d. 24 Mar 1827, Baltimore, MD
- m. Ann Pickhaver, 4 Jun 1808, Baltimore, MD
- Service: Ens., Capt. Dobbins' Co. of 39th Reg., Baltimore City Militia 16 Aug 1813 – 23 Aug 1813; and 19 Aug 1814 - 18 Nov 1814.
- Member – Robert Towles Cummins, Jr. [757 / 5076]

YEAR 2000 SUPPLEMENT
A CHRONICLE OF WAR OF 1812 SOLDIERS, SEAMEN, AND MARINES

DELARUE, Celestin
    b. Bordeaux, France
    d. Bordeaux, France
    m.
    Service: A carabinier in Capt. Pierre Roche's Co., a part of Maj. Jean Baptiste Plauche's Uniformed Btn. of Orleans volunteers Dec 1814 – Mar 1815.
    Member – Dominick Michael Valencia, Jr. [766-C / 5225-C]

DEMASS, Peter
    b. 11 Apr 1787, Duchess Co., NY
    d. 28 Sep 1872, Cayuga Co., NY
    m. Eva Elizabeth Phillips, 15 Jun 1807, Manlius, NY
    Service: Private in Lt. Samuel Tappan's Company, 23rd U.S. Infantry Reg., 9 Apr 814 – 1815; at Battles of Chippewa and Niagara (Lundy's Lane)
    Member – George Robert Demass, Jr. [754 / 5049]

DORAN, Francis
    b. ca 1767-68, Harford Co., MD
    d. after 1818, Washington Co., KY
    m.
    Service: Pvt., Capt. Garret Peterson's Co., Inf.; Ltc. Joshua Barber's 7th KY Volunteer Militia 23 Aug 1812 for 6 months.
    Member – Henry Kenneth Bowers [716-S/C / 4768-S/C]

EARECKSON, Roderick
    b. 5 Nov 1786, Queen Anne's Co., MD
    d. 1854, Queen Anne's Co., MD
    m. Caroline Winchester, 17 Feb 1814, Queen Anne's Co., MD
    Service: Sgt., Capt. John Elliott's Co., 38th Rgt., Queen Anne's Co., MD 1813.
    Member – Frederick Leif Eareckson, Jr. [781 / 5392]

ELDER, James, Sr.
    b. 25 Oct 1765, Frederick Co., MD
    d. 14 Aug 1845, Fairfield, KY
    m. Mary Ann Richards, 13 Feb 1792, Nelson Co., KY
    Service: Pvt. In Capt. Moses Shelby's Co., 1st (Lt. Col. Samuel Caldwell's) Reg., Kentucky Mounted Volunteers, 18 Sep – 30 Oct 1812.
    Member – Charles Ellwood Robertson, III [756 / 5056]

YEAR 2000 SUPPLEMENT
A CHRONICLE OF WAR OF 1812 SOLDIERS, SEAMEN, AND MARINES

FOREMAN, David
- b. 10 Apr 1791, Lexington, KY
- d. 18 Jul 1856, Pike Co., IL
- m. Margaret Galloway, 12 Dec 1808, Woodford Co., KY
- Service: Pvt., Capt. Peter Jordan's Co., KY Volunteers under Col. Joshua Barber. Enlisted for 6 months 1 Aug 1812. Due to illness, served 3½ mos.
- Member – Jerry William Zillion [769 / 5278]

GOLDSBOROUGH, William
- b. 6 May 1785, Easton, MD
- d. 14 Aug 1842, Easton, MD
- m.
- Service: Ens., Capt. Jordan's Co., Talbot Co., MD Militia, 26th Rgt. 26 Jun 1812 and 19 Oct 1814 – 20 Nov 1814.
- Member – John Seeger Kerns, Jr. [784-C / 5398-C]

HARRIS, Tyree
- b. 6 Mar 1778, Albemarle Co., VA
- d. abt. 1886, Madison Co., KY
- m. Mary Taylor, 7 Jul 1814
- Service: Sgt., Capt. White's Co., KY Mounted Volunteer Militia 18 Sep 1812 – 30 Oct 1812.
- Member – Benjamin Louis Harris [772-C / 5300-C]

HARTLEY, Richard
- b. 1784, Kent Co., MD
- d. 1832, Baltimore, MD
- m. Susanna Young, 17 Feb 1807
- Service: Pvt. in Capt. Edward Comegys' Co., 21st (Kent Co.) Regiment, Maryland Militia, 5-25 Aug 1813, 16-18 Apr, 10-13 Jul, 20 Aug-6 Sep, 11-23 Sep 1814.
- Member – Michael William Hartley [748 / 5007]

HUGHES, Benjamin
- b. 23 Feb 1789, Maryland
- d. 7 Jul 1842, Grand Gulf, MS
- m. Nancy Brashear, 6 Oct 1818, Bullitt Co., KY
- Service: Pvt. in Capt. George Trotter's Co. of Cavalry. 1st Rgt. KY Volunteer Light Dragoons 27 Aug 1812 – 31 Oct 1812.
- Member – Harry Tracy Aycock, IV [767 / 5226]

YEAR 2000 SUPPLEMENT
A CHRONICLE OF WAR OF 1812 SOLDIERS, SEAMEN, AND MARINES

HUMMER, Jacob
    b. abt. 1769, Lancaster Co., PA
    d. Oct 1854, Lancaster Co., PA
    m. Elizabeth Freymoyer, 26 Feb 1794, Lancaster, PA
    Service: Pvt., PA Volunteer Co. under Capt. Michael Petre. Service began 3 Sep 1814.
    Member – Charles Orestus Smith [773 / 5301]

ISAAC, Joseph (of Richard)
    b. 1783, Prince George's Co., MD
    d. 14 Jan 1866, Prince George's Co., MD
    m. Mary C. Williams, 26 Feb 1821, Prince George's Co., MD
    Service: Capt. 34th Rgt., MD Militia 21 Jul – 2 Sep 1813; Capt. 34th Rgt., 1st Btn. 18-24 Jun 1814 & 19-30 Jul 1814; participated Battle of Bladensburg.
    Member – Richard Barry Isaac [776 / 5331]

JACOBS, Lyman
    b. 17 Jan 1781, North Haven, CT
    d. 1 Apr 1860, New Haven, CT
    m. Ann Fosdick Kirkman, 11 May 1806.
    Service: Pvt., CT Militia, Capt. Amos Fowler's Co., Col. Benjamin Baldwin's Btn. 7 Sep 1814 – 14 Sep 1814.
    Member – Charles Pomeroy Ives, III [777 / 5342]

KEPNER, John
    b. 1788, York Co., PA
    d. Mar 1828, Franklin Co., PA
    m. Elizabeth Fehl, 1815, Adams Co., PA
    Service: Pvt. in Capt. Lindsay Sturgeon's Co., 9th Regiment, First Brigade, Fifth Division, Pennsylvania Militia, 9 Mar 1814.
    Member – Donald Joseph Wolf [755 / 5050]

LANSDALE, John Wesley
    b. 28 Jul 1791, Montgomery Co., MD
    d. 7 Nov 1836, Montgomery Co., MD
    m. Miranda Stevenson, 15 May 1815, Prince George's Co., MD
    Service: Lt., Capt. Gitting's Co., Extra Btn., Montgomery Co. Militia 26 Jul - 2 Sep 1813; Capt., 18th MD Rgt., 27 Apr 1814.
    Member – Malcolm Parker, II [760 / 5199]

YEAR 2000 SUPPLEMENT
A CHRONICLE OF WAR OF 1812 SOLDIERS, SEAMEN, AND MARINES

LEPPO, Jacob
- b. 27 Dec 1789, Carroll Co., MD
- d. 30 Mar 1862, Carroll Co., MD
- m. Susanna Miller, 10 Feb 1818, Baltimore Co., MD.
- Service: Pvt. in Capt. William Blizzard's Co., Col. Nace's (Baltimore County) Reg., Maryland Militia, 19 Aug – 10 Sep 1813.
- Member – George Duane Leatherwood Berry [746 / 4968]

LINTHICUM, Charles Griffith
- b. 10 Mar 1788, Anne Arundel Co., MD
- d.
- m. Louisa Merriweather, 15 Apr 1810, Frederick Co., MD
- Service: Adj. of 32nd MD Regt. Recruited in Anne Arundel Co., MD
- Member – George Emory Linthicum, IV [762 / 5201]

LINTHICUM, Charles Griffith
- b. 10 Mar 1788, Anne Arundel Co., MD
- d.
- m. Louisa Merriweather, 15 Apr 1810, Frederick Co., MD
- Service: Adj. of 32nd MD Regt., recruited in Anne Arundel Co., MD
- Member – John Whitaker Linthicum [761 / 5200]

LONG, Christian
- b. 1791, MD or PA
- d. Mar 1861, Carroll Co., MD
- m. Elen _____, abt 1822, MD or PA
- Service: Pvt. in Capt. William Murray's Co., 36th (Baltimore Co.) Regiment, Maryland Militia, 25 Aug – 27 Oct 1814.
- Member – Francis Brent Seville [747 / 4969]

MAULL, Henry Fisher
- b. 25 Sep 1783, Lewes, DE
- d. 11 Jan 1852, Lewes, DE
- m. Mary Bedford Webb, 19 Dec 1804, Lewes, DE
- Service: Pvt. (1813), 3rd Cpl. (1814), Capt. James J. Holland's Co., Volunteer Militia Artillery at Lewes, 3rd Bgd. under Samuel B. Davis.
- Member – Paul Marshall Long, Sr. [779 / 5357]

YEAR 2000 SUPPLEMENT
A CHRONICLE OF WAR OF 1812 SOLDIERS, SEAMEN, AND MARINES

NORTH, Hicks
- b. 20 Feb 1784, Dorchester Co., MD
- d. 7 Apr 1849, Dorchester Co., MD
- m. Eleanor Bell, 25 Dec 1815, Dorchester Co., MD
- Service: Pvt., Capt. John Brohawn's Co., 48th Rgt., Dorchester Co., 26 Aug 1814 to 29 Aug 1814; also at Battle of Ice Mound 7 Feb 1815.
- Member – Frederick Leslie Riedel, Jr. [778-C / 5356-C]

ORDRONAUX, John
- b. 6 Dec 1778, Nantes, France
- d. 24 Aug 1841, Cartagena, Columbia
- m. Jeanne Marie Elizabeth Charretton, 13 Sep 1815, Bordeaux, France
- Service: Fought as Cdr. of privateers Prince de Neufchatel & Marengo which he owned and outfitted; under letters of marque issued by US Government.
- Member – Joseph Janvier Woodward, III [775-5330]

PARR, David
- b. 27 Feb 1786, Baltimore Co., MD
- d. 8 Sept 1832, Baltimore, MD
- m. Margaret McCowan, 15 Aug 1816, Baltimore, MD
- Service: Pvt., Capt. Michael Peters' Co., 51st Rgt., Baltimore City Militia, 3rd Bgd. 23 Aug 1813 to 30 Aug 1813 & 19 Aug 1814 to 18 Nov 1814.
- Member – Frank Parr Lewin Sommerville [783 / 5397]

REEDER, William
- b. 1788, St. Mary's Co., MD
- d. 6 Jan 1853, St. Mary's Co., MD
- m. Maria Hebb, 15 Dec 1811, St. Mary's Co., MD
- Service: Cornet, Capt. Forrest's Co., 4th Cav. Dist. 16 Jun 1812; 4th Rgt. Cav. Dist. 13 Jul to 4 Aug 1813; 10 Feb to 24 Jun 1814 MD Militia.
- Member – Robinson Kendall Nottingham [780 / 5391]

ROBERTS, John (Jackie)
- b. 3 Jun 1762, Somerset Co., MD
- d. 27 Oct 1846, Somerset Co., MD
- m. Martha Roberts, 1783, Somerset Co., MD
- Service: Sgt., Capt. William White's Company, 23rd Reg. of MD, Somerset Co., 18 May to 7 Jun 1814.
- Member – Douglas Felix Ford [759 / 5118]; Roland Wilmer Ford [764-5203]

YEAR 2000 SUPPLEMENT
A CHRONICLE OF WAR OF 1812 SOLDIERS, SEAMEN, AND MARINES

ROSS, Reuben
- b. 9 Dec 1781, Baltimore, MD
- d. 9 Apr 1830, Baltimore, MD
- m. Sarah Shryer, Baltimore, MD
- Service: 2nd Lt., 1st Baltimore Volunteer Artillery under Capt. Abraham Pike, 1st Rgt. of Artillery under Ltc. David Harris.
- Member – R. Ross Holloway [770 / 5284]

SCHAEFFER, Philip
- b. 7 Jun 1770, Berks Co., PA
- d. 30 Dec 1853, Berks Co., PA
- m. Elizabeth Feterolf, 5 Sep 1797, Berks Co., PA
- Service: Pvt. in Capt. James Perle's Company, Lt. Col. Peter L. Berry's Reg., First Brigade, First Division, Pennsylvania Militia, 26 Aug 1814 – 2 Jan 1815.
- Member – Forrest Rickenbach Schaeffer [752-D / 4065]

SCHRECK, Andrew
- b. 21 Aug 1795, PA
- d. 18 Feb 1872, Crawford Co., OH
- m. Elizabeth Buffington, 23 May 1826, PA
- Service: Declaration of soldier for pension records and certificate of militia duty located in Crawford Co. Court House, 112 E. Mansfield St., Bucyrus, OH.
- Member – David Ralph Curfman, [758-D / 5094]

SMITH, William
- b. 19 Apr 1789, Philadelphia, PA
- d. 22 May 1844, Montgomery Co., NY
- m. Jane Simpson Reading, 18 Jan 1814, Montgomery Co., NY
- Service: Surgeon's Mate, Prior's Rgt., NY Militia, Plattsburgh, NY 1814
- Member – Lee Crandall Park [763 / 5202]

SMITHSON, William
- b. 1779, Harford Co., MD
- d. 3 Dec 1836, Harford Co., MD
- m. Margaret Hall Lee, 5 Sep 1805, Harford Co., MD
- Service: Pvt., Harford Co. Militia, 42nd Rgt., Capt. Joshua Amoss' Co., 29 Aug to 26 Sep 1814; Pvt., 51st Rgt., Capt. Haubert's Co., 1814.
- Member – Christopher Thomas Smithson [782 / 5393]

YEAR 2000 SUPPLEMENT
A CHRONICLE OF WAR OF 1812 SOLDIERS, SEAMEN, AND MARINES

STOVER, Daniel
- b. 1757, Franklin Co., PA
- d. Oct 1822, Franklin Co., PA
- m. Barbara Benedict, Franklin Co., PA
- Service: Pvt. in Capt. William Reese's Company, Maj. John Shauck's Detachment, Pennsylvania Militia, 31 Oct – 22 Nov 1814.
- Member – Henry Prather Laughlin [751-D / 4645]

THOMPSON, Henry
- b. 23 Jun 1774, Birmingham, England
- d. 24 Aug 1837, Baltimore, MD
- m. Ann Lux Bowley, 29 Mar 1798, Baltimore, MD
- Service: Capt. Independent Company of Horse Artillery, 3rd Brigade, 5th Cavalry District, Maryland Militia, 24 – 26 Aug 1814.
- Member – Nelson Mott Bolton [749 / 5010]

WEBSTER, Jacob
- b. 16 Feb 1786, Somerset Co., MD
- d. 15 Oct 1869, Somerset Co., MD
- m. Polly McDorman, 17 Oct 1809, Somerset Co., MD
- Service: Corporal in Capt. William White's Co., 23rd (Lt. Col. John C. Wilson's) Regiment, (Somerset Co.) Maryland Militia, 29 May – 7 Jun 1814.
- Member – Walter Edelen Webster, Jr. [753 / 5048]

WILCOX, Jehiel
- b. 2 Jul 1797, Duchess Co., NY
- d. 3 Oct 1884, Erie Co., PA
- m. Chloe Nichols, 14 Oct 1823, Sangate, VT
- Service: Pvt. in Capt. Joseph Howland's Company, Lt. Col. Solomon K. Chamberlain's Reg., Massachusetts Militia, 10 Sep – 30 Oct 1814.
- Member – Kenneth Allan Wilcox [750 / 5011]

YOUNG, William
- b. abt. 1780, Anne Arundel Co., MD
- d. abt. 1850, Howard Co., MD
- m. Jane (Jenny) Johnson, 10 Aug 1810, Anne Arundel Co., MD
- Service: Pvt. in Capt. George Stiles' Corps of Marine Artillery, Baltimore, MD from 25 Aug 1814 to 30 Nov 1814.
- Member – James Turner Young [771-C / 5299-C]

YEAR 2000 SUPPLEMENT
A CHRONICLE OF WAR OF 1812 SOLDIERS, SEAMEN, AND MARINES

MEMBER INDEX
(SUPPLEMENT)

AYCOCK, Harry Tracy, IV - 145
BERRY, George Duane Leatherwood - 147
BOLTON, Nelson Mott - 150
BOWERS, Henry Kenneth - 144
CUMMINS, Robert Towles, Jr. - 143
CURFMAN, David Ralph - 149
DEMASS, George Robert, Jr. - 144
EARECKSON, Frederick Leif, Jr. - 144
FORD, Douglas Felix - 148
FORD, Roland Wilmer - 148
HARRIS, Benjamin Louis - 145
HARTLEY, Michael William - 145
HOLLOWAY, R. Ross - 149
ISAAC, Richard Barry - 146
IVES, Charles Pomeroy, III - 146
KERNS, John Seeger, Jr. - 145
LAUGHLIN, Henry Prather - 150
LINTHICUM, George Emory, IV - 147
LINTHICUM, John Whitaker - 147
LONG, Paul Marshall, Sr. - 147
PARK, Lee Crandall - 149
NOTTINGHAM, Robinson Kendall - 148
PARKER, Malcolm, II - 146
PEICKER, Martin Jacob - 143
RIEDEL, Frederick Leslie, Jr. - 148
ROBERTSON, Charles Ellwood, III - 144
SCHAEFFER, Forrest Rickenbach - 149
SEVILLE, Francis Brent - 147
SMALLWOOD, Grahame Thomas, Jr. - 143
SMITH, Charles Orestus - 146
SMITHSON, Christopher Thomas - 149
SOMERVILLE, Frank Parr Lewin - 148
SULLIVAN, Clarence John - 143
VALENCIA, Dominick Michael, Jr. - 144
WAESCHE, James Frederick - 143
WEBSTER, Walter Edelen, Jr.- 150
WILCOX, Kenneth Allan - 150
WOLF, Donald Joseph - 146

WOODWARD, Joseph Janvier, III - 148
YOUNG, James Turner - 150
ZILLION, Jerry William - 145

OTHER NAMES INDEX
(SUPPLEMENT)

AMOSS, Joshua, Capt. - 149
BALDWIN, Benjamin, Col. - 146
BARBER (BARBEE?), Joshua, Ltc. - 144, 145
BELL, Eleanor - 148
BENEDICT, Gen. - 143
BENEDICT, Barbara - 150
BERRY, Peter L., Ltc. - 149
BLIZZARD, William, Capt. - 147
BOWEN, Amelia Milly - 143
BOWLEY, Ann Lux - 150
BRASHEAR, Nancy - 145
BROHAWN, John Capt. - 148
BUFFINGTON, Elizabeth - 149
CALDWELL, Samuel, Ltc. - 144
CHAMBERLAIN, Solomon K., Ltc. - 150
CHARRETTON, Jeanne Marie E. - 148
COMEGYS, Edward, Capt. - 145
DAVIS, Samuel B. - 147
DEWEY, Electa - 143
DOBBINS, Capt. - 143
ELDER, John, Capt., - 143
ELLIOTT, John, Capt. - 144
FEHL, Elizabeth - 146
FETEROLF, Elizabeth - 149
FORREST, Capt. - 148
FOWLER, Amos, Capt. - 146
FREYMOYER, Elizabeth - 146
GALLOWAY, Margaret - 145
GALLOWAY, Robert, Capt. - 143
GITTINGS, Capt. - 146
HARLAN, Hannah - 143
HARRIS, David, Ltc. - 149

YEAR 2000 SUPPLEMENT
A CHRONICLE OF WAR OF 1812 SOLDIERS, SEAMEN, AND MARINES

HAUBERT, Capt. - 149
HAUTZ, Magdalena - 143
HEBB, Maria - 148
HOLLAND, James J., Capt. - 147
HOWLAND, Joseph, Capt. - 150
JOHNSON, Jane Jenny - 150
JORDAN, Peter, Capt. - 145
JORDAN, Capt. - 145
KENNEDY, Col., - 143
KENNEDY, Maxwell, Col. - 143
KIRKMAN, Ann Fosdick - 146
LEE, Margaret Hall - 149
McCOWAN, Margaret - 148
McDORMAN, Polly - 150
MERRIWEATHER, Louisa - 147
MILLER, Susanna - 147
MURRAY, William, Capt. - 147
NACE, Col. - 147
NICHOLS, Chloe - 150
PERLE, James, Capt. - 149
PETERS, Michael, Capt. - 148
PETERSON, Garret, Capt. - 144
PETRE, Michael, Capt. - 146
PHILLIPS, Eva Elizabeth - 144
PICKHAVER, Ann - 143
PIKE, Abraham, Capt. - 149

PLAUCHE, Jean B., Major - 144
PRIOR, Col. - 149
READING, Jane Simpson - 149
REESE, William, Capt. - 150
RICHARDS, Mary Ann - 144
ROBERTS, Martha - 148
ROCHE, Pierre, Capt. - 144
SCARBOROUGH, Col. - 143
SHAUCK, John, Maj. - 150
SHELBY, Moses, Capt. - 144
SHRYER, Sarah - 149
SIMPSON, Jane - 149
STEVENSON, Miranda - 146
STILES, George, Capt. - 150
STURGEON, Lindsay, Capt. - 146
TAPPAN, Samuel, Lt. - 144
TAYLOR, Mary - 145
TROTTER, George, Capt. - 145
WEBB, Mary Bedford - 147
WHITE, Capt. - 145
WHITE, William, Capt. - 148, 150
WILLIAMS, Mary C. - 146
WILSON, John C., Ltc. - 150
WINCHESTER, Caroline - 144
YOUNG, Susanna - 145

www.ingramcontent.com/pod-product-compliance
Lightning Source LLC
Chambersburg PA
CBHW052100230426
43662CB00036B/1716